The Punch Book of Women's Rights

by the same author

**WOMEN'S SUFFRAGE AND
PARTY POLITICS 1866-1914**

The Punch Book of Women's Rights

Constance Rover

SOUTH BRUNSWICK
NEW YORK: A. S. BARNES AND COMPANY

Library of Congress Catalogue Card Number: 70-83509

SBN 498 07503 6

Printed in the United States of America

Dedicated to the memory of
DAME MILLICENT GARRETT FAWCETT
1847-1929

Contents

Bibliographical Note

A formal bibliography is neither necessary nor possible, the only publications (apart from *Punch*) mentioned being:

Austen, Jane, *Pride & Prejudice*, Lond. 1813
Farr, Wm., *Vital Statistics*, Lond. 1885
Fawcett, Millicent Garrett, *The Women's Victory – & After*, Lond. 1920
Patmore, Coventry, *The Angel in the House* (Poem), Lond. 1854

For those interested in the women's emancipation movement, the classic work is:

Strachey, Ray, *The Cause*, Lond. 1928

This book is unfortunately out of print but a welcome recent addition to the literature on the subject, covering the same ground but with an extension to modern times is:

Kamm, Josephine, *Rapiers & Battleaxes*, Allen & Unwin, 1966

A Bibliography covering the various aspects of the women's movement, by Professor O. R. McGregor, was published in the *British Journal of Sociology* in March, 1955. The books mentioned in this Bibliography may be obtained from the Fawcett Library, Wilfred Street, S.W.1, which is a specialized library devoted to all aspects of the history and current activities of women and which contains both original records and a vast number of printed books. Publications since 1955 which may be considered to have particular relevance include the following:

Fulford, Roger, *Votes for Women*, Faber & Faber 1957
Hobman, D. L., *Go Spin, You Jade*, C. A. Watts 1957
Kamm, Josephine, *Hope Deferred*, Methuen 1965
Pankhurst, Christabel, *Unshackled*, Hutchinsons 1959
Rover, Constance, *Women's Suffrage & Party Politics* 1866–1914, Routledge & Kegan Paul 1967

The last mentioned work contains a bibliography of the women's suffrage movement.

Although outside the main period of the campaign, the following book:

Mitchell, David, *Women on the Warpath*, Jonathan Cape 1966

which deals with women's activities in the first world war, provides a background which does much to explain the change of attitude that made women voters acceptable in 1918.

Acknowledgements

I am greatly indebted to *Punch* for their generosity in allowing me research facilities on their premises and in particular to their librarian, Miss Elisabeth Bower. I am conscious that any merit this work may possess is due primarily to the excellence of the cartoons, which are reproduced by the courtesy of *Punch*.

Like all workers in the field of the women's emancipation movement, I owe a lot to the Fawcett Library and its Librarian, Miss Vera Douie, o.b.e., whose knowledge of the subject is unrivalled.

I am also grateful to the Principal and Governors of the North-Western Polytechnic, London, for without the facilities for basic research provided by them in the past, I should have lacked the background knowledge which has enabled me to embark upon this relatively light-hearted effort.

Finally, I must pay tribute to my husband; like nineteenth century *Punch* he is 'no great women's rightist' but he has gallantly put up with my absorption in the subject.

Constance Rover

Highgate,
London N.6.

Introduction

Introduction

Dame Millicent Garrett Fawcett, leader of the constitutional movement for women's suffrage, wrote of the period before the first world war:

> 'For quite a number of years we had had true and faithful friends in . . . *Punch*, and other papers. The latter gave us a series of first-rate pictures and cartoons, which I hope one day may be reproduced as *Punch's* "History of Women's Suffrage".'[1]

It is to meet this wish, on the centenary of the foundation of the movement to which Mrs. Fawcett (as she was known throughout the campaign) gave such distinguished leadership, that the present book has been compiled. The scope of the work has been extended to cover some other aspects of the 'Women's Rights Movement' but I feel sure Dame Millicent would not mind, as she was interested in the whole campaign and made an important contribution to the struggle for education.

She always enjoyed a joke and quoted, with appreciation, *Punch's* verse:

[1] *The Women's Victory—& After* by Millicent Garrett Fawcett, p. 78 (Sidgwick & Jackson, 1920).

'You speak, Mr. Asquith, the suffragist said,
    Of the Will of the People wholesale;
But has the idea never entered your head
    That the People are not wholly male ?'[1]

In the nineteenth century, however, *Punch* was not
quite so friendly to the women; it shared the conventional view of their rôle in society and usually showed
the 'Women's rightists' as unattractive, aggressive and
mostly be-spectacled types. It felt that pretty young
women should not bother their heads with learning
but nevertheless was prepared to give credit where
credit was due. On the occasion of Philippa Fawcett
(Dame Millicent's daughter) being placed above the
Senior Wrangler at Cambridge in the examination
results of 1890, congratulations were published:

'Punch, whose especial care is
    To sever truth from sham
Is no great Women's Rightist;
    But *this* is not clap-trap;
Of pundits the polightest,
    To you he lifts his cap!
Docteur en Droit, Punch watches
    Miss FAWCETT by the Cam.'   *21.6.1890*

One does not normally turn to a humorous journal
for advanced Radical thought, though *Punch* is excep-
tional in being strongly Radical in its early years (a
position to which it has reverted in modern times) and
a political even more than a humorous weekly. Most
of the material about women's rights comes in *Punch's*

[1] *The Women's Victory—& After* by Millicent Garrett
Fawcett, p. 78 (Sidgwick & Jackson, 1920).

more conventional, middle period and a certain conservatism in its attitude towards the subject is understandable, as the odd or *avant garde* is necessarily comic. One obtains, however, a much more balanced idea of the period by scanning the pages of *Punch* than through reading feminist literature; it is helpful to be made to realize how different the average woman of the mid-nineteenth century was from the advanced, high-minded, middle-class Radical ladies, often of Unitarian or Quaker stock, who formed the early group of feminists.

Most of the problems which the women's rights movement set out to solve are portrayed clearly in the pages of *Punch*. Ever quick to resent injustice, *Punch* shows sympathy for the bitter poverty and miserable condition of governesses and seamstresses, while poking fun at the fatuity of the life of the well-to-do young lady. There are some aspects of Victorian life, however, which *Punch* chooses to ignore. It was always a respectable journal which could be left about the Victorian house without any fear of the morals or sensibilities of the most refined young lady being adversely affected. An integral part of the women's emancipation movement was Josephine Butler's campaign against the Contagious Diseases Acts; the unsavoury subject of prostitution kept on cropping up but this, understandably, was seldom referred to, although the problem of poverty which contributed towards it is clearly shown and in 1843 *Punch* published Thomas Hood's celebrated 'Song of the Shirt', written in anger on learning that a seamstress was paid 'five farthings' for the labour of sewing a shirt.

By the twentieth century, *Punch* seems to have developed a soft spot for the women fighting for the vote; it mocks them very gently and is much more caustic towards their political opponents. It shares the widespread exasperation at the way in which Asquith's government handled the women's claim.

As may be imagined, once the Pankhursts arrived on the scene, the suffragettes provided a fertile source of comedy. There are so many excellent cartoons in this period that a selection only can be reproduced. 1913 was a bumper year.

The campaign for women's rights is an important aspect of social history from the 1850s until the first world war. Like many other campaigns, the steam went out of it on achieving a fair measure of success but before its objectives had been completely attained. The pages of *Punch* illuminate the movement in an inimitable way.

The Problem

The Problem

The problem which aroused the compassion of the early feminists was that of the 'female supernumeraries' as *Punch* called them. The comfortable assumption that every woman ought to marry and be maintained by her husband just did not fit the facts of the mid-nineteenth century. In January 1848, *Punch* (quoting from the *Plymouth Times*) points out that there were 'forty single ladies for every single man' in Weston-super-Mare. Even in the age-group where there were most married women, between 35 and 40, a quarter of the women were single.[1] *Punch* gives 'A Series of Views' on 'Our Female Supernumeraries' at the beginning of 1850:

> '*The Alarmist View.* If the surplus female population with which we are overrun increases much more, we shall be eaten up with women. What used to be our better half will soon become our worse nine-tenths; a numerical majority which it will be vain to contend with and which will reduce our free and glorious constitution to that most degrading of all despotisms, a petticoat government.'

[1]See the analysis of the 1851 census in *Vital Statistics*, by William Farr, p. 46. (1885).

The Needlewomen at Home and Abroad

AT HOME   ABROAD

12.1.1850

In *The Cynical View*, *Punch* gives a favourite, but somewhat shortsighted remedy of the time:

'All our difficulties arise from a superabundance
of females. The only remedy for this is to pack
up bag and baggage, and start them away.'

The remedy of emigration is emphasized in *The
Domestic View*, where *Punch* says:

'The daughters of England are too numerous and
if the Mother cannot otherwise get them off her

hands, she must send them abroad into the world.'

The message is repeated by cartoon and by *Our Own View*:

'It is lamentable that thousands of poor girls should starve here upon slops, working for slopsellers, and not only dying old maids because dying young, when stalwart mates and solid meals might be found for all in Australia. Doubtless they would fly as fast as the Swedish henchaffinches – if only they had the means of flying. It remains with the Government and the country to find them wings.'   *5.1.1850*

As Punch was prepared to admit, most of the 'female supernumeraries' lacked the means of flying, and, indeed, emigration was a factor which increased the disparity between the sexes, as it was easier for a man to emigrate than for a woman. This disparity applied particularly to the middle classes where, to the male emigrants, was added a considerable number who undertook limited periods of service overseas. Apparently anything which could dispose of some women was welcomed in that light. It comes as a shock to find that Florence Nightingale's magnificent effort in organizing nurses for the Crimean War inspired a *Punch* cartoon, *How to Get Rid of an Old Woman*. One's sense of outrage is, however, mitigated when one realises that the 'old woman' is Lord Aberdeen, the prime minister, who was mishandling the war.

Punch shared the general view that it was the duty of a woman to marry and kept plugging the suggestion that if a husband could not be found at home, he could be found abroad, quoting news items such as the following:

HOW TO GET RID OF AN OLD WOMAN.

28.10.1854

'Out of the female immigrants who recently arrived at Melbourne by the *William Stewart*,
eight were married within 24 hours after their
landing.'   *16.12.1848*

An article in August, 1848, shows that a needlewoman's return for ten hours' labour could be as little
as 2½d. (*A Shroud as well as a Shirt*) and another the
following month on *The Sempstress at Home* points out
that the Union (Workhouse) or Gaol would be pre-
ferable. In 1850 *Punch* reports that the *Chronicle* had
opened a list of names and addresses of London
needlewomen, commenting that the payment of those
engaged might include 'the possible luxury of an
incidental chop, to vary the dietry of thrice-drawn
tea-leaves and butterless bread'.

This destitution was blamed for the wide-spread
prostitution of the times, usually ignored by *Punch* but
sometimes referred to, as in the penultimate verse of
The Needlewoman's Farewell:

'Now speed thee, good ship, over sea, and bear
    us far away,
    Where food to eat, and friends to greet, and
    work to do await us –
Where against hunger's tempting we shall not
    need to pray –
    Where in wedlock's tie, not harlotry, we
    shall find men to mate us.'   *12.1.1850*

No doubt husbands were waiting for the small
minority of working-class women who were willing
and able to emigrate but the average middle-class
woman was unfitted by her upbringing for the hardships of colonial life. The early feminists who came to
the aid of governesses found that the only ones whom
it was safe to send overseas were those who were well-
equipped; in other words, those for whom work could

probably have been found at home.

Punch realized that the roughness of frontier life might not appeal to the Victorian woman of refinement and comments:

'*Matrimonial destitution at the Diggins.* According to the latest intelligence from California, there are scarcely any ladies there. Amidst all the riches, therefore, of that El Dorado, the treasure of a charming wife, it seems, would be sought in vain. Probably lovely women will never emigrate to California for gold, so long as there is enough of the precious metal at home to make a little hoop that will just go round the fourth finger of the left hand.'   *8.6.1850*

While the problem of poverty was one that affected the working-classes generally and was to some extent taken for granted, middle-class spinsters could be reduced to destitution also, to the embarrassment of their relations. There was little the middle-class woman could do, lacking means of support, but attempt to obtain a place as a governess or companion. Many of the early feminists, living in the South of England, lacked knowledge of factory conditions and the hardships of factory life, but it was difficult to ignore the situation of governesses, for nearly all middle-class families contained at least one member who had been reduced to that condition. Articles and cartoons on the parlous situation of the governess run through the pages of nineteenth-century *Punch*, little sign of improvement being shown as time went on, in spite of the successes of the Women's Rights Movement. Governesses, as well as being what *Punch* termed 'Sisters of Misery', had to suffer the indignity of being figures of fun as well. Their lot was frequently worse than that of the domestic servant. Neither fish nor fowl, they were poised uneasily between 'the family' and the

CONSIDERATE—VERY!

Master George (alluding to the New Governess, who happened to be within hearing). 'CROSS, DISAGREEABLE OLD THING, I CALL HER!'

Miss Caroline. 'OH GEORGY! BUT WE OUGHT TO GIVE WAY TO HER; RECOLLECT, DEAR, SHE'S A VERY AWKWARD AGE!'

22.10.1864

servants' hall. Soured by their experiences and their
'come down' in life, it is not surprising that some of
them were disagreeable.

In 1848 *Punch* vouches for the authenticity of an
advertisement and application form from the principal
of an Academy on the banks of the Humber.

> 'Mrs. —— begs to inform Miss —— that she
> wishes for a lady who will be able to instruct a
> class of about ten little boys about three hours
> daily; to give instruction to her two daughters in
> needlework; to superintend the washing and
> dressing of Mr. ——'s pupils, and to assist at
> table and in the wardrobe department. These
> objects are paramount. Other valuable services
> would receive due consideration. The salary
> proposed is not less than £20, nor more than £40
> per annum. £2 allowed for travelling expenses.
> The lady to pay her own laundress. Mrs. ——
> trusts to engage one whom she may have the
> pleasure of associating with, and that the con-
> nection may be lasting. If Miss —— will fill up
> the enclosed form as well as she is able, and return
> it, a definite answer shall be given without delay.
> Number of pupils about thirty.'

Punch proceeds to quote the application form, giving
suggested answers.

> 'Have you had experience in teaching children?
> During what time? In schools or families, or how
> long in each?'
>   (For some years a teacher in the School of
>   Adversity; can be well recommended by suf-
>   fering.)
> 'What branches of learning do you profess to
> understand?'
>   (To carve a joint with no waste of fat; and to make

tea upon tea-leaves as strong as the first pot.)
'Have you had much practice in plain needlework?'
(A good deal of plain work; having made shirts
for 3d. a piece, before reduced to the condition
of governess. . . .)
'Are you now, and have you generally been, in
good health?'
(Most happily constituted for the situation.
Lungs of iron, flesh of granite, and heart of
lead: otherwise, should not presume to apply for
the appointment.)   *15.7.1848*

Over forty years later, the same sort of abuse was
being disclosed. In 1890, under the heading 'A White
Slave', *Punch* quotes a news item from the *Daily News*
of June 12:

'Miss HARKER took service as a day governess
in a family at Stockton, at a salary of 25s. a month,
coupled with the privilege of dining in the house.
She found herself under the necessity of taking a
lodging, the rent for which more than absorbed her
modest stipend. She taught three children English
and music. Afterwards a couple of infants were
placed in her charge. Nor was that all, for when
the servants left, the new governess had "to cook
the dinner, wash the dishes, and clean the knives".
After this she asked for a holiday, the result being
that "she was shown the door". Thereupon she
brought an action in the County Court for a
month's salary in lieu of notice. Judgement for the
plaintiff with costs, payable forthwith.'

Punch pilloried this disgraceful example of exploitation with a set of verses:

'Poor Miss HARKER went to Stockton, to
    Stockton on the Tees,
But not to make her fortune, or to loll at home at
    ease;
She went to be a governess, and hoped, it would
    appear,
To board and lodge and dress herself on £15
    a-year.

A lady once informed us how a lady can be
    dressed
As a lady all for £15, and in her very best;
But she never would have ventured to include in
    her account,
The lodgings and the breakfasts too for this
    immense amount.

Now life may be a river, as Pactolus was of old,
Which brings you lots of water to a minimum of
    gold,
But sometimes it were better, when the water
    sinks so low,
That it fails to turn your mill-wheel, if the river
    ceased to flow.

So all day long with urchins three Miss HARKER
    toiled in chains,
And she poured the oil of learning well upon
    their rusty brains,
And she practised them in music, and she
    polished up their sense
With the adverbs and the adjectives, and verbs
    in mood and tense.

And they said, "She's doing nicely, we will give
    her something more
(Not of money, but of labour) ere we show her
    to the door,
Why, we've got two baby children, it is really
    only fair
That Miss HARKER should look after them,
    and wash and dress the pair.

"And, Miss HARKER, it will save us such a lot
    of trouble too.
If, when our servants leave us, they can leave
    their work to you
So you'll please to cook our dinner, let your
    motto be *Ich Dien*,
(No, no, you needn't thank us) and you'll keep
    our dishes clean.

"And, of course, you'll do it daily – what was
    that you dared to say?
You would like to rest a week or so, and want a
    holiday?
Who ever heard such nonsense? Well, there's
    one thing we can show,
Not politeness, but the door to you – Miss H.
    you'd better go."

So she went, but brought her action, and I'm
    thankful to relate
That when the case was argued she hadn't long
    to wait.
"Costs and judgement for the plaintiff, the
    defendants' case is fudge,
Pay her monthly wage, she's earned it and
    deserves it," said the Judge.

There be Englishmen in England, sleek men, and
    women too,
Who tie their purse-strings tighter than tradi-
    tion's grasping Jew.
What care they for fellow-feeling, who for profit
    try to lure
Fellow creatures to their grindstone for the faces
    of the poor?

And they set some wretched slave to work her
    fingers to the bone,
Then sullenly deny her bread, or give at best a
    stone;
And after she has grubbed and scrubbed, they
    insolently sneer
At one who dares to ask for rest on £15 a-year.'

21.6.1890

NO REASONABLE
OFFER REFUSED

A SKETCH FROM NATURE.

12.7.1884

The indignity of the position of the Victorian spinster, either as an unwanted dependant in the home of a
relative or struggling to maintain herself by her own
efforts in a situation where there was little scope for
her to earn a decent living, meant that marriage or,
rather, the finding of a husband, was a very serious
business. In spite of the contemporary hazards of
frequent child-bearing and a high maternal mortality
the Victorian young woman (frequently pushed by her
mother) rushed into matrimony. In doing so, she lost
most of her legal rights but a husband was a meal
ticket; he might also be an object of affection but even
if, like Mr. Collins in Jane Austen's *Pride & Prejudice*
he was 'neither sensible nor agreeable', at least the
ignominy of spinsterhood would not have to be en-
dured. The only single women likely to find satisfaction
in 'single blessedness' were those wealthy enough to be
able to maintain themselves in comfort in their own
establishments. The *Punch* cartoon showing 'No

A LAMENT

Dowager. 'IT'S BEEN THE WORST SEASON I CAN REMEMBER, SIR JAMES! ALL THE MEN SEEM TO HAVE GOT MARRIED, AND NONE OF THE GIRLS!'
15.11.1884

A POTENTIAL SON-IN-LAW

Anxious Mother of Many Daughters. 'PAPA DEAR, *DO* GET MRS. LYON HUNTER TO INTRODUCE YOU TO HIS HIGHNESS; YOU MIGHT THEN ASK HIM TO CALL, YOU KNOW.'
Papa Dear. 'WHAT FOR?'
Anxious Mother. 'WELL, MY LOVE,—YOU KNOW THE CUSTOM OF HIS COUNTRY!—HE MIGHT TAKE A FANCY TO SEVERAL OF THE GIRLS AT ONCE!'
20.2.1875

Reasonable Offer Refused' applied to most young
women of the period. No doubt there were a few who
enjoyed the sustained campaign, partly a game of skill
and partly a gamble, whereby the middle- or upper-
class woman tried to capture a husband of status.
Punch gives excellent advice to those playing this game
in 'The Young Girl's Companion' by Mrs. Payley.
On 'The Choice of a Husband', Mrs. Payley advises:

> 'Any woman, my dear young girls, can marry any
> man she likes, provided that she is careful about
> two points. She must let him know that she would
> accept a proposal from him, but she must never
> let him know that she has let him know. The
> encouragement must be very strong but very
> delicate. To let him know that you would marry
> him is to appeal to his vanity, and this appeal never
> fails; but to let him know that you have given him
> the information is to appeal to his pity, and this
> appeal never succeeds. Besides, you awake his
> disgust. Half the art of the woman of the world
> consists in doing disgusting things delicately. Be
> delicate, be indirect, avoid simplicity, and there
> is hardly any limit to your choice of a husband.'
>
> *21.5.1892*

Compared with this, the attainment of a higher
degree at one of our universities sounds like child's
play. It seems a pity that those who had the technique
for such a game were so soon out of it and that they
could not subsequently use their technique for some
other game, such as big business.

This necessity for husband-hunting and the contemporary idea that 'accomplishments' made a girl
attractive but that 'learning' would destroy her appeal
led to another problem of the period; the ignorance of
practically all young women and the frivolity of certain

COUNTRY-HOUSE STUDIES
(HABITS OF THE YOUNG LADY VISITORS)
'A HAIR-BRUSHING.' WHICH MEANS, PRETTY DRESSING-GOWNS,
AND GOSSIP IN EACH OTHER'S ROOMS, FOR ANY NUMBER OF
HOURS, AFTER SAYING 'GOOD NIGHT!' DOWN-STAIRS
(N.B. Only confidential Friends admitted.)   *23.11.1867*

sectors of society. Appreciation of this problem was
not confined to the feminists but tended to be shared
by all serious-minded women; the feminists concentrated mainly on the need for single women to be
educated to maintain themselves while their more
conservative sisters felt that girls should be trained for
marriage rather than just to catch husbands. The
futility of the life of the Victorian young lady was to
drive Florence Nightingale almost out of her mind
before she managed to break away from it. As might
be expected, the pointlessness of much of contemporary social life and the follies of fashion were frequently put before the readers of *Punch*, the theme

GENTLE TEMPTATION
'NOT COME WHILE WE ARE SO GAY? O! BUT THERE'S NOTHING
ON JUST NOW, I ASSURE YOU! TO-MORROW, THERE WILL ONLY
BE THE PARK IN THE MORNING, AND THEN SOME PEOPLE COME
TO LUNCHEON, AND, AFTERWARDS, MAMMA WANTS ME TO GO
AND PAY VISITS WITH HER AND DO SOME SHOPPING, AND YOU
WON'T MIND LADY MUFF TO FIVE O'CLOCK TEA, AND WE MAY
POSSIBLY GO TO THE FLOWER SHOW FOR AN HOUR OR TWO.
THERE WILL ONLY BE TEN AT DINNER, AND WE SHAN'T LEAVE
FOR AUNTY'S DANCE UNTIL LONG AFTER YOUR BED TIME,
YOU KNOW, GRANDMA DEAR!'   24.5.1873

running all through the nineteenth century. The caption for the cartoon, 'Gentle Temptation' (24.5.1873)
gives some idea of the life of a well-brought-up young
lady of the period. Commenting on the society girl of
1890, *Punch* states:

'. . . By their (her parents') example she has been
taught to hold as articles of her very limited faith,
that the serious concerns of life are of interest only
to fools, and should, therefore (though the infer-
ence is not obvious), be entirely neglected by

herself, and that frivolity and fashion are the twin
deities before whom every self-respecting woman
must bow down.

Having left the Seminary at which she acquired an
elementary ignorance of spelling, a smattering of
French phrases as used by English lady novelists...'

15.3.1890

Victorian prosperity, combined with a plenitude of
domestic service, and the movement of many processes,
formerly performed at home, to the workshop or
factory, had largely robbed the middle-class woman
of her former economic functions. The lady, who ought
not to soil her hands, had emerged. (Indeed, she
frequently wore gloves in the house.) For a woman to
work who did not need to was looked upon as taking
bread out of the mouths of the hungry.

The feminist revolt was a middle-class rebellion
against interrelated evils; many women needed work,
but could find it, if at all, at starvation wages only;
women were mostly ignorant and unfit for worthwhile
employment; convention limited them to a few overcrowded occupations; the more fortunate women who
wished to help were hampered through lack of political
influence, as they were unenfranchised; the married
woman's legal personality was merged in that of her
husband; in certain sectors of society women were
encouraged to be frivolous and irresponsible and then
despised for becoming what they had been trained to
be.

The Women's Rights Movement

The Women's Rights Movement

By the 1850s the position of men as the 'Lords of Creation' was being challenged and *Punch's* Almanack for 1853 is devoted to 'The Ladies of the Creation', showing a reversal of the traditional rôles of the sexes.

Some progress has been made on both sides of the Atlantic; American women, annoyed at their exclusion from participation in the World Anti-Slavery Convention in London (England) in 1840, had organized themselves; a small, local Convention on Women's Rights was held at Seneca Falls in 1848 and a somewhat larger, national Convention at Worcester, Massachusetts, in 1850. In England, a limited Infants' Custody Act was passed in 1839, largely as the result of Caroline Norton's agitation, giving mothers some rights over children under seven. (*Punch* supported Lord Chelmsford's Bill to extend this Act in 1873 and provided an Obituary Notice, in verse, for Caroline Norton in 1877.) A Governesses' Benevolent Institution was formed in 1841 and some progress had been made in the education of women and girls. The 1850s saw the commencement of the campaign for married women to hold property and the formation of a Society for the Promotion of the Employment of Women.

Married women, in particular, lacked legal rights

Mary protecting the weaker sex

Punch Almanack 1853

THE WOMAN AT THE WHEEL.

Punch Almanack 1853

in the mid-nineteenth century; if they had any earnings, these legally belonged to their husbands, as did their property, in default of a marriage settlement. The working woman could obtain little protection from the Courts and cases of brutality were all too common; the right of a woman to live apart from her husband was not established until 1890 (Regina v. Jackson). *Punch* was always quick to resent injustice and in 1848 scarified the system which gave a man the option of £5 or two months hard labour for beating a woman round the head with a stone in a handkerchief, while imposing one month's hard labour without option because a policeman was slightly hit with the same stone.

Understandably, *Punch* was more concerned about women suffering from brutality than those demanding opportunity but, in truth, their cause was one and the same; the whole status of women needed raising. In 1855, during the Crimean War, with its accompanying

THE PARLIAMENTARY FEMALE

Father of the Family. 'COME, DEAR; WE SO SELDOM GO OUT TOGETHER NOW—
CAN'T YOU TAKE US ALL TO THE PLAY TONIGHT?'
Mistress of the House, and M.P. 'HOW YOU TALK, CHARLES! DON'T YOU SEE
THAT I AM TOO BUSY. I HAVE A COMMITTEE TO-MORROW MORNING, AND I HAV[E]
MY SPEECH ON THE GREAT CROCHET QUESTION TO PREPARE FOR THE EVENIN[G]'

Punch Almanack 18[__]

Russophobia, *Punch* was complaining, '. . . it does not appear that even a Muscovite serf is accustomed to thrash his wife with quite the frantic ferocity of the British blackguard'.

In May, 1874, this point of view was put in verse:

Woman's Wrongs
'There's preaching from platforms and fighting of
    fights
By our sisters who shriek for "Woman's Rights",
But of Punch's sympathy more belongs
To his sisters who suffer from "Woman's
    Wrongs".

Her wrongs who must daily and nightly cower,
In the sway of a brute with a tyrant's power,
Who in sickening fear of her life must go
From the killing kick and the blinding blow.

Who, with all her sex's burdens, must weep
'Neath the weight of all man's strength can heap
On backs that their load at his will must take,
And hearts that, if they can't bear, may break.

And more power to Colonel Egerton Leigh
And more speed to the day *Punch* hopes to see,
When, woman's wrongs done away to begin,
Her "rights" are all that is left to win.'   *30.5.1874*

These verses did not point to an isolated incident; in an imaginary examination paper for the wives of working men, *Punch* asks in October of the same year: 'What is the best defence in fights where hob-nailed boots are freely used?' A few months later, *Punch* highlights a particularly brutal case by cartoon and verse.

'WOMAN'S WRONGS'

BRUTAL HUSBAND. 'AH! YOU'D BETTER GO SNIVELLIN' TO THE 'OUSE O' COMMONS, YOU HAD! MUCH THEY'RE LIKELY TO DO FOR YER! YAH! READ THAT!'

'MR DISRAELI.—There can be but one feeling in the House on the subject of these dastardly attacks—not upon the weaker but the fairer sex. (*A laugh*). I am sure the House shares the indignation of my hon. friend who will, I hope, consider he has secured the object he had in view by raising the question. * * * Assuring my hon. friend that Her Majesty's Government will not lose sight of the question, I must ask him not to press his Motion further on the present occasion.'—*Parliamentary Report Monday May* 18.   *18.5.1874*

The Rough's Last Wrong

'They may well say old England is battered,
    I wonder where changes may stop,
Now Bigwigs of the Bench have not faltered
    To let us down *this* hawful drop?
Bad enough the cat's brutal correction,
    In our gaols should be let to run rife,
Spite of LORD ABERDARE'S wise objection –
    BUT A MAN HANGED FOR KILLING HIS WIFE!

And in Lancashire, too, where poor fellers
    Brass-tipped clogs have the habit to use;
Where fam'lies is crowded in cellars,
    And the corner-men look down on shoes
How's a family's 'ead to keep order,
    Or put down aggrawation and strife,
If a few broken ribs is called murder,
    AND A MAN HANGED FOR KILLING HIS WIFE?

Now I axe, is an 'ome worth a copper,
    With them 'Spectors and Boards free to come?
Is wives wives, as you mayn't fetch a topper
    With a stick not so thick as your thumb?
There's spoons as wants law for the dumbest
    Of dumb things, 'tis true, on my life;
But of all starts, this last start's the rummest
    A MAN HANGED FOR KILLING HIS WIFE!'

                                        16.1.1875

Only the more imaginative and perceptive could see
the connection between the working woman, sometimes
ill-treated by her husband, and the middle-class woman
demanding individual rights; the opponents of women's
rights were apt to say that the law, as it stood, pro-
tected women, while the feminists insisted they would
never have justice under man-made law and that they

A REAL HARD CASE
(THE ROUGH'S LAST WRONG.)
Liverpool Ruffian ''ERE'S A GO!—A MAN 'ANGED FOR
KICKIN' HIS WIFE TO DEATH! I SHALL 'AVE TO TAKE
MY BOOTS OFF!'   *16.1.1875*

needed to share in the law-making process. The mid-
Victorian feminists could show that women, rightless
in so many respects, were deemed legally able to
consent to their own debauchery at the tender age of
thirteen; not until W. T. Stead's revelations in the
Pall Mall Gazette scandalized the nation (*The Maiden
Tribute of Modern Babylon*) was the age of consent
raised to sixteen by the Criminal Law Amendment
Act of 1885.

In the nineteenth century *Punch* often (though not
always) subscribed to the conventional idea that a
woman interested in 'Women's Rights' must be unattractive and an oddity; she was usually portrayed
as a vinegary spinster or the domineering wife of a
hen-pecked husband. (See the women in the front

row of Mrs. Lyon Hunter's Drawing-Room, p. 51.)

'The rights of Women who demand,
    Those women are but few:
The greater part had rather stand
    Exactly as they do.

Beauty has claims, for which she fights
    At ease, with winning arms;
The women who want women's rights
    Want, mostly, Woman's charms.'   *19.2.1870*

A considerable number of remarkably good-looking women were associated with the feminist movement, from the golden-haired and handsome Barbara Leigh-Smith (Mme Bodichon) of the *Englishwoman's Journal* to the beautiful and elegant Emmeline Pankhurst. *The Englishwoman's Journal* was started in 1857 and Jessie Boucherett (later to become associated with it) recounts how she visited the offices, expecting to find some dowdy old lady, and was amazed to find herself amongst well-dressed, beautiful and gay young women. Other early feminists associated with the *Englishwoman's Journal* included Bessie Rayner Parkes (Mrs. Belloc), Emily Faithfull and Adelaide Anne Proctor. Talented additions in 1869 to the 'Langham Place Group', as it was sometimes called, were Emily Davies, later to become the leading figure in the struggle for the higher education of women, and Elizabeth Garrett, later Dr. Elizabeth Garrett Anderson. This group of women was associated with the formation of a Ladies Discussion Society, or 'Kensington Society', set up in 1865, the first Women's Employment Bureau, a Ladies' Institute with a reading room and club, the Female Middle Class Emigration Society and the Victoria Press (for printing the *Journal*). One of the group, Miss Isa Craig, became assistant secretary to the Association

EXTREMES THAT MEET
AT MRS. LYONS CHACER'S 'SMALL AND EARLY.'
Fair Enthusiast. 'LOOK! LOOK! THERE STANDS MISS GANDER
BELLWETHER, THE FAMOUS CHAMPION OF WOMEN'S RIGHTS,
THE FUTURE FOUNDER OF A NEW PHILOSOPHY! ISN'T IT A
PRETTY SIGHT TO SEE THE RISING YOUNG GENIUSES OF THE
DAY ALL FLOCKING TO HER SIDE, AND HANGING ON HER LIPS,
AND FEASTING ON THE SAD AND EARNEST UTTERANCES
WRUNG FROM HER INDIGNANT HEART BY THE WRONGS OF HER
WRETCHED SEX? O, ISN'T SHE *DIVINE*, CAPTAIN DANDELION?'

Captain Dandelion (of the 17th Waltzers). 'HAW! 'FAIR OF TASTE, YOU
KNOW! WATHER PWEFER *SHE*-WOMEN MYSELF—WATHER
PWEFER THE WRETCHED SEX WITH ALL ITS WONGS—HAW!'
Mr. Millefleurs (of the 'Ess Bouquet' Club). 'HAW! WATHER A GWUBBY,
SKWUBBY LOT, THE WISING YOUNG GENIUSES! HAW-AW-AW!!'
14.3.1874

for the Promotion of Social Science. Of course, the
women associated with the movement came in all
shapes and sizes; the plump, be-spectacled Lydia
Becker, early leader of the suffrage campaign, was a
gift to the cartoonists. What all the women had in
common was a basic seriousness of purpose and dis-
satisfaction with at least some aspects of the position
of women. *Punch* was willing to laugh at the women's
detractors as well as the 'strong-minded females'.

Early cartoons were composed in the form of captions, often so extended that they read rather like a short story, to which some unfortunate artist had to add a drawing. One (not reproduced) shows a massive and handsome young woman beside a man half her size and is called 'A Discussion on Women's Rights'. The caption reads:

> 'Sir Hercules Fitzanak admits that women occasionally rival men in intellect and character, but contends that their inferiority in strength and stature will prove an insuperable bar to their ever being placed on a footing of equality with the sterner sex. Miss Millicent Millefleurs says, nothing, but thinks a great deal.'   *24.7.1875*

Punch, in 1870, devotes over half a page to an open letter to Mrs. Professor Fawcett (Millicent Garrett Fawcett) gently chiding her for her feminist activities, which are attributed to her wish to keep up with her 'excellent and irrepressible husband'. This letter conveniently summarizes the various aspects of the 'Women's Rights Movement' as, 'Women's Suffrage Movement, Women's Separate Property Movement, Women's Examination Movement, Women's University Movement, Women's Admission to the Professions Movement, etc.' (16.4.1870). The tone of the letter is typical of the relatively friendly opponent of 'Women's Rights'. *Punch* asks Mrs. Fawcett,

> 'Has it never occurred to you that in parcelling out life in two great fields, the one inside, the other outside the house-doors, and in creating two beings so distinct in body, mind and affections as men and women, the Framer of the Universe *must* have meant the two for different functions?'

In *Punch*, as elsewhere, God is shown to be distinctly anti-feminist.

An early success in the campaign for women's rights was the attainment (or, as the women insisted, the restoration) of the Municipal vote in 1869, on the same property qualification as men. The movement for 'separate property' was set back by the establishment of a Divorce Court in 1857, as the Court was able to give help to an injured wife, but the cause revived, mainly under the leadership of Elizabeth Wolstenholme (later Mrs. Wolstenholme-Elmy), and Married Women's Property Acts were passed in 1870, 1874 and 1882. *Punch* notes this latter (Consolidation) Act in 'Punch's Fancy Portraits No. 4', picturing the Rt. Hon. Osborne Morgan, M.P. '. . . vide his Married Women's Property Act . . . just the man for the ladies'.

By degrees, women became more active in public affairs. They were elected to School Boards in 1870 and the first woman Poor Law Guardian was elected in 1875. *Punch* noted, in 1876, that two ladies had come forward as candidates for the St. Pancras Board of Guardians, commenting:

'The Guardianship of the Poor will doubtless be mitigated for them by an admixture of the softer sex with the harder. Boards of Guardians comprising Ladies may be expected to include Guardian Angels.'   *15.4.1876*

PUNCH'S FANCY PORTRAITS.—No. 104.

RIGHT HON. OSBORNE MORGAN, M.P.

The various Acts relating to Local Government, from the setting up of County Councils in 1888 onwards, further enlarged the sphere of women and in 1906 *Punch* referred to a Bill which had been drafted to allow women to sit on local bodies, commenting '. . . and not a moment too soon. Many local bodies badly want sitting on.'   *7.10.1882*

Throughout the period, a useful 'platform' for the

women's movement was provided by the National
Association for the Promotion of Social Science. In
1874 *Punch* reported:

Social Science for the Ladies

'It is said that next year a section of the Social
Science Congress will be entirely devoted to
Members of the Fair (or rather unfair) Sex.'

The experience gained through participating in the
activities of the Association was of great value to the
feminists; reports of the Congresses and pamphlets
published by various branches of the Association
provided favourable publicity for the women's movement.

The opponents of women's rights made much of
women's privileges, claiming that these should go by
the board if equal rights were demanded. This was
reasonable, if it could be assumed that the privileges
and courtesies were all on one side. It is amazing how
much was made of the kindly (but not vitally important) custom of a man giving up his seat to a
woman, the subject of more than one *Punch* cartoon.
The theme of the 1875 cartoon, where the youth in
Mrs. Lyon Hunter's drawing room refuses to give up
his seat to a believer in the equality of the sexes, is
repeated in another well-known cartoon (not reproduced) of 1882. This latter cartoon shows a number
of people in a 'bus and the caption reads:

'Old Gent (mildly) "Pray, are you an advocate of
Woman's Rights, Ma'am?"
Lady (sharply) "Most certainly I am, Sir. Why
do you ask?"
Old Gent "Because I was about to offer you my

'EVIL COMMUNICATIONS,' &C.
SCENE—Mrs Lyon Hunter's Drawing-Room, during a Lecture on 'Women's Rights'.
Modest Youth (in a whisper, to Young Lady looking for a Seat). 'ER—EXCUSE ME, BUT DO *YOU* BELIEVE IN THE EQUALITY OF THE SEXES, MISS WILHELMINA?'
Young Lady. 'MOST *CERTAINLY* I DO, MR JONES.'
Modest Youth. 'HAW! IN THAT CASE OF COURSE I NEEDN'T GIVE YOU UP MY CHAIR!' *18.12.1875*

seat; but of course you claim the right to stand!"'

Most modern women who travel on the London Underground find that this latter right has been fully awarded to them, but it is not as new as one thinks. *Punch* was complaining in 1897 that men did *not* give up their seats to women in third class carriages on the North London Line. ('A Word for the Women', 29.11.1879.)

Reverting to the idea that courtesies and 'services rendered' were not entirely confined to the male sex, *Punch* remarks:

'. . . Did we say three words would emancipate womenkind? One word would—monosyllable. They might refuse . . . to sew on buttons; in short, might strike altogether. Women could obtain all their rights, and a great deal more, if they would only make up their minds to say "No".'

11.5.1872

This was asking far too much when women's whole status and position depended on men and when, in addition to the reasonable acceptance of family obligations, women had been indoctrinated with the idea that it was their duty to please men. A *Punch* cartoon, 'A Discussion on Woman's Rights' (not reproduced) makes this point. 'Algernon' is shown surrounded by women and the caption reads:

'Algernon (to his Sisters, his Cousins, and his Aunts).

"My dear creatures, if you want equality among the sexes, you must learn to be independent of us as we are of you. Now we men live chiefly to please ourselves first, and then each other; whereas you women live entirely to please *us*!"'

31.12.1881

Punch pays tribute, from time to time (usually at their death) to outstanding women of Victorian days whose achievements or philanthropy made them famous. Although not 'feminist', the veneration in which these women were held helped to raise women's status. Amongst them were Florence Nightingale, Mary Carpenter of the 'Ragged Schools' and Baroness Angela Burdett Coutts, the philanthropist. Of Mary

Carpenter *Punch* writes, on her death in 1877:

> "Twas she first drew our city waifs and strays
>   Within the tending of the Christian fold,
> With eyes of love for the averted gaze
>   Of a world prompt to scourge and shrill to
>   scold.'   *30.6.1877*

Few of the nineteenth century feminists claimed that identity with men which their opponents attributed to them; indeed, many felt men were the superior sex; nevertheless, they held that 'The Subjection of Women' (as John Stuart Mill entitled his celebrated book) was a shameful thing.

GOING IN FOR WOMEN'S 'LEFTS'
Confidential Friend (to elderly and not unattractive Spinster).
'SO, DEAR, YOU'VE GIVEN UP ADVOCATING WOMEN'S RIGHTS?'
Elderly Spinster. 'YES, I NOW GO IN FOR WOMEN'S LEFTS.'
Confidential Friend. 'WOMEN'S LEFTS! WHAT'S THAT?'
Elderly Spinster. '*WIDOWERS*, MY DEAR!'   *22.1.1881*

The Struggle for Education

The Struggle for Education

The Governesses' Benevolent Institution was formed in 1841 and the philanthropists and feminists associated with this enterprise soon realized that girls' education provided an example of the blind leading the blind. If the status and pay of the governess was to be raised, some means of training her must be found. The Rev. Frederick Denison Maurice of King's College, London, started a series of lectures for governesses and other young women, which resulted in the opening of Queen's College for Women in 1848. Noted educational pioneers who were trained there included Frances Mary Buss, founder of the North London Collegiate School, and Dorothea Beale, Principal of Cheltenham College. Some six months later, in 1849, Bedford College for women was opened. Although called 'Colleges', both Queen's and Bedford were more like secondary schools, taking girls over twelve as well as women.

About a decade later, another educational pioneer made her début; Emily Davies, the daughter of a country parson, met the Rev. Maurice and Barbara Bodichon (who had studied at Bedford College) on a visit to London. She became interested in the women's movement generally and education in particular and was later to carry through the fight for the higher

WHAT WE HOPE TO SEE
'PRUDES FOR PROCTORS, DOWAGERS FOR DONS, AND SWEET GIRL GRADUATES.'
Tennyson.   *Punch Almanack 1866*

education of women and to found Girton.

The feminists were undoubtedly right in giving
priority to education. As Emily Davies pointed out,
it was no wonder that women who had not learnt to do
anything could find nothing to do. If women were to
be worthy of 'rights', education was a prime necessity.
Current thought included the idea that arithmetic was
'too severe for females' and that Latin and Greek
might be beyond the compass of the feminine men-
tality, which is why Emily Davies was determined that
girls should receive the same training as boys and sit
the same examinations. In contrast, Dorothea Beale did
not wish to see girls compete in examinations and
there were many who felt that the subjects studied by
girls should not parallel those of boys' schools. In the

REAL EDUCATION
MR PUNCH IS OF OPINION THAT A POLITE AND EASY BEARING
TOWARDS THE OPPOSITE SEX (TEMPERED, OF COURSE, WITH
PROPRIETY AND DISCRETION) CANNOT BE INCULCATED AT
TOO EARLY AN AGE. HE THEREFORE RECOMMENDS THAT
WHENEVER AN INSTITUTE FOR YOUNG LADIES HAPPENS TO
MEET AN ACADEMY FOR YOUNG GENTLEMEN, THEY SHOULD
ALL BE FORMALLY INTRODUCED TO EACH OTHER, AND AL-
LOWED TO TAKE THEIR WALKS ABROAD IN COMPANY. *15.6.1872*

event, both schools of thought contributed to the
educational advance of men and women alike; com-
petitive examinations of the traditional kind scotched
the idea that women could not compete with men on
their own ground and the widening of syllabuses to
include studies of a more liberal nature, thought to be
suitable for girls and women, was ultimately of benefit
to boys and men. This latter result was stimulated by
the North of England Council for the Higher Education of Women, promoted by Anne Jemina Clough and
Josephine Butler to provide lectures for older girls and

'SWEET GIRL-GRADUATES' ... AFTERNOON TEA versus WINE
Punch Almanack 1873

women. At the Council's request, a special examination
for women was arranged by Cambridge University in
1869. This examination, with a more liberal syllabus
than was customary, was thrown open to men five
years later and became the 'Higher Local Examination'. The lectures promoted by the North of England
Council were very successful and soon became merged
in the University Extension Scheme.

The pages of *Punch* reflect a variety of contemporary
attitudes to women's education. The stereotype of the
severe-looking female is there, with the idea that brains
and beauty are incompatible; the female professor who
is so attractive that she puts the male students off their
stroke is also to be found, together with genuine
tributes to women, such as Philippa Fawcett, who
achieved academic distinction. There was a slight

justification for the idea that a learned woman was unlikely to be a great beauty. The attainment of a high standard of elegance is a time-absorbing occupation and no woman pursuing high academic standards could afford the time (even if she had the interest) to attain the standard of the 'professional beauty' who, in those days of elaborate toilets would (with the help of a lady's maid) achieve impressive results.

The women's movement records a middle-class struggle, although early feminine philanthropists such as Hannah More and Mary Carpenter had tried to bring some education to the working classes. In reading about the women's movement, one is apt to forget that there were state-sponsored educational projects, even before the Act of 1870. Apparently the teachers in the State system were not in the same parlous position as the governesses and *Punch*, quoting from a government pamphlet issued by Mr. Chadwick, throws an amusing sidelight on the general picture. The pamphlet deals with schoolteachers in government Schools of Art and the extract quoted reads:

> 'The females have been so far advanced in mental power and influence as to have been *lost to the service* by matrimonial engagements obtained with exceeding rapidity. To avoid these losses plainer candidates were selected for training, but they too have obtained preference as wives *to a perplexing extent*.'
> 9.6.1855

Faced with the same problem in our schools, this item is probably more amusing to us today than it was to *Punch* readers of the time; *Punch* simply draws the moral that apparently beauty is a secondary consideration in choosing a wife, but to the modern mind, the idea of selecting women on account of their plainness and the eminent Mr. Chadwick's subsequent perplexity is hilarious.

The contemporary debate, recently revived by Sir
John Newsom, on whether girls' education should be
related to their future function as wives and mothers,
was foreshadowed in an article in *Punch* in 1874.

A Girls' School in the Kitchen
'A Cambridgeshire Vicar', writing in the *Times*,
truly remarks that 'The Art of cookery, under
the auspices of MR. BUCKMASTER, is now assum-
ing the place which it ought to hold among the
accomplishments of English Ladies'. It is, indeed,
satisfactory to see the agitation for Women's Rights
accompanied by a movement in the cultivation of
their duties. Let the accomplishment of cooking
be as generally studied by girls as that of music is,
and the results of learning the one will probably
prove in general a good deal more satisfactory than
we find those of instruction in the other. The
majority of our wives and daughters will be
enabled to dress a dinner as well as they can dress
themselves, and perhaps better than they dress
their hair; and there will no longer be room for
the unkind, if not altogether uncalled for remark,
that there are not many bread-winners whose wives
are able to make bread sauce.' *18.4.1874*

The feminists wanted something more than this and
prominent amongst supporters of the women's cause
were Professor Henry Fawcett, later to become
Gladstone's Postmaster General, and his wife Millicent
(neé Garrett). Henry Fawcett (in spite of being blind)
was able to combine his academic work at Cambridge
with his position as M.P. for Brighton. *Punch*, in
November 1874, has an item under the heading,

Learning for Ladies
'Charming Mr. Punch,

O DO see what that darling MR. FAWCETT said the
other day about us Ladies:

"I venture to assert, with no little confidence, that
the more a woman's mind is trained, the more her
reasoning faculties are developed, the more
certainly does she become a suitable companion for
her husband; she is better able to manage his house
with tact and skill and to obtain the best, the most
tender and the most enduring influence over her
children."

Isn't that *nice* of him? Only I think he rather
jumps to a conclusion when he assumes that
husbands are so monstrously intelligent and
mentally well trained. Of course he fancies this,
else why say that the more a wife is educated the
more suitable a companion to her husband she
becomes? I'm sure I'm not *over* clever, but I
reckon I'm a match for *my* husband at any rate;
and although my reasoning faculties may not be
much developed, I should like to catch him trying
to argue any point with me when I have made up
my mind.

Yours, Mr. Punch, admiringly—and also MR.
FAWCETT'S.

Xantippe Sophonsiba Greymare
(nee BOUNCER)

P.S. I'm not much of a *manager* in common
household matters; but I fancy that my husband
would acknowledge that I manage *him* effectively.'

7.11.1874

This article is, perhaps, a timely reminder that few
people lived in the high-minded Radical circle fre-
quented by Professor and Mrs. Fawcett and that the
education of the average man left much to be desired.
Nevertheless, Professor Fawcett was helping the
women's cause when he tried to make men see that

A TURK!

The Colonel. 'AS FOR WHAT THEY CALL *"INTELLECT"*, AND THAT SORT OF THING, WHY, WHAT *I* SAY IS, THE LESS OF IT IN A *WOMAN* THE BETTER, MY BOY!'

Little Tomkyns. '*MY* SENTIMENTS TO A T, SIR! *INTELLECT*, INDEED! AS FOR *ME*, I'VE ALWAYS LOOKED UPON WOMAN AS *A MERE TOY!*'   *15.11.1872*

an educated wife would be a more interesting companion than one whose ideas were entirely restricted to 'women's sphere'.

Typical of the conventional reaction, which is shown periodically in the pages of *Punch*, are the following verses:

> *Nursery Rhymes for the Times*
> 'Sally was a pretty girl
>   Fanny was her sister;
> Sally read all night and day
>   Fanny sighed and kissed her.
>
> Sally won some school degrees
>   Fanny won a lover;
> Sally soundly rated her,
>   And thought herself above her.
>
> Fanny had a happy home,
>   And urged that plea only;
> Sally she was learned—and
>   Also she was lonely.'   *20.2.1875*

Turning to the struggle for admission to the Universities, the opening of Girton is noted by *Punch* in November, 1873 with a quotation from the *Echo:*

'The College for Women at Cambridge is now established, Girton College having been opened at Cambridge this week, and the tutorial staff, with their girl students, are now in residence and have commenced the collegiate year.'   *1.11.1873*

The following issue of *Punch* suggests the inaugural lecture should be on 'Winter Fashions', other subjects suggested including 'The Plain Joint', 'Patchwork' and 'Washing at Home'. Nevertheless, the successes of girls in the Oxford and Cambridge Local Examinations, which had been formally opened to them in 1865, and the establishment of Girton made an impact; *Punch*, in December 1874, reports the remarks of the Chairman at a meeting held in Hanover Square on Women's Suffrage:

'Since that time (when John Stuart Mill first introduced the subject to the House of Commons in 1866) the tone of the press had very greatly changed, and the old argument of women's intellectual weakness had dwindled down into the much less formidable one of her physical weakness.'
                                        19.12.1874

The resolution for women's suffrage at this meeting was proposed by Miss Rhoda Garrett; all the Garrett sisters were prominent workers for women's rights, Millicent Garrett Fawcett and Elizabeth Garrett Anderson becoming the most eminent.

In 1875 the opening of Newnham followed that of Girton and *Punch* is prepared to admit that women might, in the future, become professors. It is even

TERRIBLE RESULT OF THE HIGHER EDUCATION OF WOMEN!
MISS HYPATIA JONES, SPINSTER OF ARTS (ON HER WAY TO
REFRESHMENT), INFORMS PROFESSOR PARALLAX, F.R.S., THAT
'YOUNG MEN DO VERY WELL TO LOOK AT, OR TO DANCE WITH,
OR EVEN TO MARRY, AND ALL THAT KIND OF THING!' BUT
THAT 'AS TO ENJOYING ANY RATIONAL CONVERSATION WITH
ANY MAN UNDER FIFTY, *THAT* IS *COMPLETELY* OUT OF THE
QUESTION!'   *24.1.1874*

prepared to concede that women professors might be
attractive but not that attractiveness could be combined
with sound scholarship. In 'The Professor of the
Future', the first verse runs:

> 'The Lady Professor's so wondrous wise,
>   Her very face is a *study*;
> She mounts a pair of celestial blue eyes
>   And her mouth's small ellipsis is ruddy.'

The third verse rather spoils the tribute,

> 'Her small white hand has a clenching force
>   If sometimes her facts look like fiction;
> And whate'er be the logic of her discourse,
>   Her smiles breed instant conviction.' *6.11.1875*

Nine years later, *Punch* commemorated the successes of Newnham and Girton with verses addressed to 'The Woman of the Future'. The first and last verses are quoted below:

'The Woman of the Future! She'll be deeply read,
    that's certain,
With all the education gained at Newnham or at
    Girton;
She'll puzzle men in Algebra with horrible
    quadratics,
Dynamics, and the mysteries of higher mathe-
    matics;
Or, if she turns to classic tomes a literary roamer,
She'll give you bits of HORACE or sonorous lines
    from HOMER.

O pedants of these later days, who go on undis-
    cerning,
To overload a woman's brain and cram our girls
    with learning,
You'll make a woman half a man, the souls of
    parents vexing,
To find that all the gentle sex this process is
    unsexing.
Leave one or two nice girls before the sex your
    system smothers,
Or what on earth will poor men do for sweet-
    hearts, wives and mothers?'   *10.5.1884*

This idea of 'overloading a woman's brain' was a tiresome one to combat, especially when there were medical 'experts' to suggest there might be dire physical consequences. Eventually it was decided that the best thing to do was not to meet the challenge head-on but to launch a flanking attack and Dr. Elizabeth Garrett Anderson proclaimed that the chief reason for poor health in girls and young women was lack of proper exercise, not brain-work. This line of propaganda proved to be very fortunate, for it was taken up with enthusiasm by girls' schools and colleges and led to the inclusion of games and exercises in their curricula, to the untold benefit of the students' health. *Punch* approved of this development, part of a set of verses addressed to 'Girl Gymnasts' reading:

'Let the Ladies learn gymnastics, if they please, as
    well as men,
Alternating feats athletic with the pencil and the
    pen;
They'll improve too pale complexions, and their
    eyes will shine as stars,
After practice on the ladders and the horizontal
    bars.'
                                    8.3.1884

Many nineteenth-century women undoubtedly suffered from inadequate exercise and tight-lacing, but side-by-side with these one sees, in the pages of *Punch*, intrepid horsewomen, taking fences with verve and leaving their escorts behind. Mr. Punch could be rather a Philistine at times and did not seem to object to athletic women in the way he disliked learned women. A sonnet in 1876 expresses his general attitude:

Sonnets for the Sex
'We like the lady who rides, rows or rinks,
But not the lady who makes pious fuss,
Or she-philosopher who thinks she thinks,

And studies Sanskrit or the Calculus
Or hunts midst *Polypi* for missing links.
When these appear, we ask why this is thus?'
                                    17.6.1876

In 1878 London University opened its degrees to women and in 1882 *Punch* quotes the following report from *Nature:*

> 'A novel feature at the meeting of Convocation of London University was the appearance, for the first time, of Female Graduates in Academic costume.'

Punch goes on to celebrate the event in rhyme:

> 'Girl Graduates! They realize
> Our TENNYSON'S old fancies,
> And winning Academic prize,
> They scorn seductive dances.
> Here come the feminine M.D.s
> Of physic fair concocters,
> Who write prescriptions with such ease,
> The "violet-hooded Doctors".'   *3.6.1882*

A couple of years later, *Punch* records that at the half-yearly meeting of the University of London, 'Lady Graduates' for the first time took part in the proceedings.

> 'Thus Woman wins. Haul down your flag,
>   Oh, stern misogynist before her.
> However much a man may brag
>   Of independence he'll adore her.
> Traditions of the bygone days
>   Are cast aside, old rules are undone;
> In Convocation Woman sways
>   The University of London.'   *19.1.1884*

Reverting to Cambridge, the University would not consider awarding its degrees to women. It was first

Why shouldn't Girton Rink, when Cambridge Rows? *15.4.1876*

approached in 1880, after Charlotte Scott of Girton
had been bracketed with the eighth wrangler in the
Mathematical Tripos list, and again in 1888, following
the success in the previous year of Ageneta Ramsay,
also of Girton, who had secured a first class placing
in the Classical Tripos, none of the men of that year
being placed higher than second. In 1890 Cambridge
women were so successful that *Punch* termed it 'The
Ladies Year'. It seems most appropriate that the
honour of being placed above the Senior Wrangler fell
on Philippa Fawcett, daughter of Henry and Millicent
Fawcett. Philippa was a Newnham student and sat for
the Mathematical Tripos, gaining the most celebrated

'PLACE AUX DAMES!'

(Following the brilliant success of Miss FAWCETT at Cambridge, Mlle. BELCESCO, a Roumanian lady, took her degree to-day as *Docteur en Droit*. Like Miss FAWCETT, she obtained the highest place at the examination for the Licentiate's Degree, and her success was not less brilliant at the examination for the Doctor's Degree.—'*Daily News*' *Paris Correspondent*.)

'SENIORA FAWCETT'

So to be entitled
henceforth, as she is
Seniorer to the Senior
Wrangler.
To Seniora
FAWCETT,
The Wranglers
yield first place;
And now, first of the
Law set,
One of another race,
Beauty, Brunette,
Roumanian,
From man takes top
Degree!
In learning's race
Melanion
Is beaten, one can
see,
By the new Atalanta;
At Law School or
Sorbonne,
As at our native
Granta,
The girls the prize
have won.
Bravo, Brunette
Belcesco!
Some Limner ought
to draw
A quasi-classic fresco,
O Lady of the Law!
O Mathematic
Maiden!
And show the pretty
pair

With Learning's
trophies laden
And manhood in a
scare.
Ah, *Portia* of Paris!
Urania of the Cam!
Punch whose especial
care is
To sever truth from
sham,
Is no great Woman's-
Rightist,
But *this* is not
clap-trap;
Of pundits the politest,
To you he lifts his
cap!
Docteur en Droit,
Punch Watches
Miss FAWCETT
by the Cam;
To you she quick
despatches
A friendly telegram.
He, friend of all the
Nations,
Of Woman as of
Man,
Adds his
'felicitations'.
Well done,
Roumanian!

mathematical honour in the world, although the man placed immediately below her became Senior Wrangler. In the same year Margaret Alford, a Girton scholar, was bracketed with the senior classic, the combination of the two results destroying the idea that mathematics and the classics were male preserves.

In two successive issues, *Punch* paid tribute to these results and also to the success of Mlle Belcesco, a Roumanian woman who had qualified as Doctor of Law at the Sorbonne. Apparently Philippa Fawcett wired congratulations to Mlle Belcesco.

Tennyson seems to have been popular with *Punch* during this period and there are frequent references to 'A Dream of Fair Women' and 'Sweet Girl Graduates'. Further verses celebrating the Cambridge successes run:

' "A Dream of Fair Women"—who shine in the
    Schools,
The Muse should essay ere her ardour quite cools.
Come, hands, take your lyres and most carefully
    tune 'em,
For Girton in glory now pairs off with Newnham.
Miss FAWCETT the latter with victory wreathed,
And now, ere the males from their marvel are
    breathed,
Miss MARGARET ALFORD, the niece of the Dean,
As a Classical First for the former is seen.
Let Girton toast Newnham, and Newnham
    pledge Girton
And—let male competitors put a brisk "spurt" on,
Lest when modern Minerva adds learning to
    grace,
Young Apollo should find himself out of the race.'

                               28.6.1890

Punch's attitude towards the higher education of
women, like that of the general public, continued to be
ambivalent. The tributes to the Cambridge girls are
followed from time to time by a hankering after the
'dear old days' such as the lines to 'A Fair Philosopher':

'Ah! Chloris! be as simple still as in the dear old
    days;
Don't prate of Matter and free Will,
And IBSEN'S nasty plays.
A girl should ne'er, it seems to me,
Have notions so pedantic;
'Twere better far once more to be
Impulsive and romantic.'   *23.1.1892*

In spite of their successes, women had to wait until
1948 to be admitted to Cambridge degrees on equal
terms with men.

    Developments at Oxford were not dissimilar to those

ST. VALENTINE'S DAY AT GIRTON
First Young Lady (opens Valentine, and reads):— " ''Ερως ἀνίκατε μάχαν
"Ερως, ὃς ἐν κτήμασι πίπτεις
CHARMING, ISN'T IT? GUSSIE MUST HAVE SENT IT
FROM OXFORD?'
Second Young Lady (overlooking). 'YES, IT'S OUT OF THE
ANTIGONE—THE LOVE-CHORUS, YOU KNOW. HOW
MUCH JOLLIER THAN THOSE SILLY ENGLISH VERSES
FELLOWS USED TO SEND!'   *26.2.1876*

at Cambridge, though somewhat in arrear. Successful
lectures for ladies were followed by the setting up of
two halls of residence. There was a dispute as to
whether or not these should be connected with the
Church of England, with the result that in 1879,
Somerville was set up on an undenominational basis
and Lady Margaret Hall with a Church of England
connection. Oxford preceded Cambridge by opening
its degrees to women in 1920.

Provincial, Scottish and Irish universities extended
their degrees to women during the nineteenth century,
the last to do so being Durham in 1895.

The struggle for the education of girls and women
was won in the nineteenth century, in spite of some
inequalities still persisting. From 1870 onwards the
state extended elementary education to girls on the
same terms as boys; the feminists and their supporters
had made it possible for middle-class girls to receive an
education, rather than a training in 'accomplishments';
the 'siege of Cambridge' and the successes of the
women students had opened the universities.

Women and Work

Women and Work

In the mid-nineteenth century women who worked for money were mainly employed in domestic service, agriculture, mills and factories, or as seamstresses or governesses. Some of the employment was seasonal in nature, such as work in agriculture or that of London seamstresses, who were in great demand during the London season. The feminists saw the problem as that of widening the scope of women's employment, so that the workers were not all competing within a few, overcrowded occupations, a change which could only be accomplished if women were better educated and trained. Most women made unsatisfactory shop assistants, as they had had little or no training in arithmetic and could not add up the cost of the sales. (We may have met one or two of these, before the cash register took over.)

In working to enlarge the fields of employment, the feminists had to fight the reluctance of a section of the public to admit there was a problem at all – were not women maintained by men? – and a widespread belief that female capacity was too limited for women to embark upon fresh kinds of work. Most accounts of the women's emancipation movement include the story of Louisa Garrett (the eldest of the Garrett sisters) asking her hairdresser if hairdressing would not be a suitable employment for women, to be met with a horrified denial of the possibility, as it had taken HIM (the hairdresser) a fortnight to learn the trade. In so far as trade unions were successful in protecting the rights of their male members, this was an additional obstacle. The obstacles, however, were not so strong as the forces working in women's favour during the nineteenth century. The expansion of trade and commerce with the consequent need for clerks, together with new inventions such as wireless telegraphy and the typewriter, provided new fields of employment for women who were increasingly obtaining at least an elementary education and sometimes, in the middle classes, a reasonable secondary schooling. One of the first new fields to be opened to respectable women was nursing, largely through the efforts of Florence Nightingale. She was not very interested in 'women's rights' but the distinction of her achievements helped the women's cause.

The feminists' efforts were concentrated in two main streams; one, as indicated above, was the attempt to widen employment generally and in this connection the 'Society for Promoting the Employment of Women' was formed by the group of enterprising Radical ladies associated with the *Englishwoman's Journal* (see p. 46 ante); the other was the storming of the professions which had been male preserves, the most spectacular being the attempt to enter the medical profession.

Punch's favourite remedy for destitute women, emigration, was taken up by Maria Rye, who found that the only class of woman which could obtain a free or assisted passage to the colonies was domestic servants. Together with Jane Lewin, she founded the 'Female Middle Class Emigration Society' in 1862 (later the 'British Women's Emigration Association'). Maria Rye discovered that travelling on a ship carrying emigrants was a hazardous business; there were many deaths during the voyage because conditions were so bad, and those surviving were wont to arrive at their destination sick and exhausted.

Punch was sympathetic towards women needing work and in 1874 paid a tribute to Emily Faithfull, who had founded the Victoria Press, with women compositors, in 1859 (see p. 46 ante), and continued to work for the employment of women.

> 'An old and faithful worker in the cause of women (EMILY of that ilk) has started a weekly paper which, if it keeps up to its purpose and its promises, deserves *Punch's* support and that of all friends of the feebler and fairer, softer and sweeter, willinger and weaker, worse-used and worse paid, harder-worked and harder-thrashed, sex (*Punch* is bound to add, in fairness, and under his breath, the nagginger and nastier when it chooses). MISS FAITHFULL calls her paper *Women & Work*, its object being to make known the work to the women who want it, and the women to the work that wants them. *Punch* can only wish good speed to the woman and her work; for it is sorely needed.'   *13.6.1874*

At about the same time Mrs. Emma Paterson formed the Women's Protective and Provident League with the object of helping women to form their own trade unions. Some were formed but the movement was not a great success. Emma Paterson's efforts towards the admission of women into the established men's trade unions proved of greater benefit. In the state of under-employment prevailing even in the 'boom' periods of the nineteenth century, it was often the fact that women were under-paid and unorganized, and therefore undercut the men, which gave them employment at all; women were cheap labour.

Where many people think the feminists went wrong was in their resistance to protective legislation. There had been a series of Factory Acts limiting the hours of work of women, children and young persons and in 1842 women were excluded from underground work in the mines, as the result of the unhealthy and deplorable conditions disclosed by Lord Shaftesbury's Commission. Many of those dismissed from the coal mines could find no alternative employment and starvation was not very good for their health either.

One can see the feminists' point of view, which was largely that of the mid-century political Radicals; women were classed with children and young persons as in need of protection and were restricted in a way which men were not. With hindsight, one can see that the Factory Acts did good to both men and women; indeed, the men were accused of hiding behind the women's skirts, as it was usually uneconomic to keep the factories working for the sake of the men only and the reduction of women's hours led to a much-needed reduction of factory hours generally. The freedom to bargain supposed to be possessed by the working-man was a myth, unless he had the protection of a union behind him; there was a permanent reservoir of un-employed, even in boom times, and who wants freedom to starve?

Henry Fawcett was one of those who opposed restrictions on women's employment with, of course, the highest motives. As Gladstone's Postmaster General he facilitated women's work in the Post Office and when he died on 6th November 1884 *Punch* honoured him with flattering obituary verses.

Modern feminists still campaign for the removal of restrictions on women's employment. They argue that women would not wish to work in steel works and at the coal face but that there should be no legal

LADY-PHYSICIANS.
WHO IS THIS INTERESTING INVALID? IT IS YOUNG REGINALD
DE BRACES, WHO HAS SUCCEEDED IN CATCHING A BAD COLD,
IN ORDER THAT HE MIGHT SEND FOR THAT RISING PRAC-
TITIONER, DR ARABELLA BOLUS!   *23.12.1865*

prohibition. The restriction on night work in factories,
they contend, sometimes works against women's
interests. In the affluent society and the welfare state
where women are not forced through destitution into
unsuitable jobs it would seem more sensible to concentrate on making all types of work safe and healthy
rather than to preclude women from certain kinds of
work or hours of working. After all, who objects to
nurses doing night work?

The story of the assault upon the medical profession
is that of two women becoming registered medical
practitioners by slipping in through the back door, as
one might say, and then a prolonged struggle to enter
the front door. Elizabeth Blackwell was born in London
but her family moved to America, where she qualified
as a doctor in 1849. Her name was placed on the British

OUR PRETTY DOCTOR
Dr Arabella. 'WELL, MY GOOD FRIENDS, WHAT CAN I DO FOR YOU?'
Bill. 'WELL, MISS, IT'S ALL ALONG O' ME AND MY MATES BEIN' OUT O' WORK, YER SEE, AND WANTIN' TO TURN AN HONEST PENNY HANYWAYS WE CAN; SO, 'AVIN' 'EARD TELL AS *YOU* WAS A RISIN' YOUNG MEDICAL PRACTITIONER, WE THOUGHT AS P'RAPS YOU WOULDN'T MIND JUST A RECOMMENDIN' OF *HUS* AS NURSES.'   *13.8.1870*

Medical Register in 1859 and the following year the medical profession secured a new charter enabling it to refuse registration to holders of foreign degrees. *Punch* took a friendly interest in Miss Blackwell's career. In 1848 an item headed 'A medical Maiden' records her attendance as a medical student at Boston and suggests that this would make her a good wife and mother. In 1849 she is shown graduating in New York.

The second woman to enter through the back door, after a struggle, was Elizabeth Garrett, later Dr. Elizabeth Garrett Anderson. She was inspired to seek medical training through hearing a lecture by Elizabeth Blackwell on the suitability of the medical profession for women and with her father's help applied to the hospitals and Schools of Medicine for training but without success. She compromised by entering Middlesex Hospital as a nurse in 1860 where, after a while, she was allowed to attend the lectures, but she made the mistake of gaining top marks in an examination, which led to the male students petitioning against her, with the result that she was banned from the lectures. With considerable ingenuity, Elizabeth planned to advance on two fronts; she worked at general subjects in the hope that London University would allow her to matriculate so that she would be qualified, if the chance ever came, to embark on the course for the M.D. degree. This proved fruitless, as the University barred her from matriculation on account of her sex. Her second venture proved more successful, although it was far from what she wanted. Elizabeth had found that the Society of Apothecaries was legally unable to prevent her from sitting their examination, which she easily passed, and that this carried with it a licence to practice. Both Elizabeth and her father felt this qualification inadequate, so it was necessary to look overseas. Permission was obtained for Elizabeth to sit for the Paris M.D. without living in Paris; she studied for and passed the necessary examinations, which included surgery, and received her degree in 1869, her name being put on the British Medical Register not by virtue of her Paris M.D. but by reason of her Apothecaries' licence.

This deplorable event lead to another door being locked. Four other women had passed the preliminary examination of the Apothecaries' Society by this time but steps were taken to see that by the time they were sufficiently advanced to qualify, it was impossible for them to do so.

One might have thought the success and efficiency of the two Elizabeths would have made the frontal attack upon the medical profession easy, but this was not the case. The main assault was made by a group

THE COMING RACE
Doctor Evangeline. 'BY THE BYE, MR SAWYER, ARE YOU
ENGAGED TOMORROW AFTERNOON? I HAVE RATHER
A TICKLISH OPERATION TO PERFORM—AN AMPU-
TATION, YOU KNOW.'
Mr Sawyer. 'I SHALL BE VERY HAPPY TO DO IT FOR
YOU.'
Dr Evangeline. 'O, NO, NOT *THAT*! BUT WILL YOU
KINDLY COME AND ADMINISTER THE CHLOROFORM
FOR ME?'   *14.9.1872*

of young women, Sophia Jex-Blake being the most
outstanding, who attempted to train at Edinburgh
University. One has, perhaps, to go to the Civil Rights
Movement in America to find scenes at a University
comparable to those which took place in Edinburgh in
1870 when male students resorted to mud-slinging and
jostling to exclude the women and, on one occasion,
pushed a sheep into a lecture room where the women
were sitting. The University establishment presented
more dignified but more effective opposition to the
women. Clinical Instruction in the Infirmary was
necessary but was denied them. The University Court
eventually proposed that the women should be allowed
to finish their medical education if they would re-
linquish their demand for graduation, but the 'certi-
ficate of proficiency' proffered instead was worthless,

THE FEMININE 'FACULTY'
New Housemaid (to her Master). 'O, SIR! I'M GLAD YOU'VE COME IN.
THERE'S A PARTY A WAITIN' IN THE SURGERY TO SEE YOU'.
(It was Mrs Dr Mandragora Nightshade, who had called professionally about
'a Case.') 'HE—SHE—WOULD COME IN, SIR,—AND—I THINK'
(shuddering) 'IT'S A MAN IN WOMAN'S CLOTHES, SIR!!!'   *24.5.1873*

as it was impossible to practice without a degree.
Punch, although not progressive in this matter and
sharing the prevalent Victorian prudery which felt
mixed medical classes were impossible, eventually
became infuriated at the way in which the women were
treated. In 1874 *Punch's Essence of Parliament* records:

'Then MR. COWPER-TEMPLE moved to fit the Scotch
Universities for Female Students.
Edinburgh *did* admit a batch of Ladies to the
Medical Classes, and then refused them its degrees.
Think as we may about women's education, that
was bad logic.
One real difficulty – apart from the question of

32. Dr. Meilanion Jones, finding himself outstripped in the race for patients by the fair Doctor-
ess Atalanta Robinson, gallantly throws her a wedding ring and wins the day.

Punch Almanack 1877

sex – is the want of teaching power for separate
classes for ladies. Mixed Medical Classes are
impossible. This DR. PLAYFAIR pointed out. But
PLAY-FAIR, of all men, is bound to remember that
fair-play is a jewel, and the women have not had
fair-play in this matter. It should be looked to,
and means taken to settle the matter one way or
the other. If women are not to be admitted to
Medical Classes and Degrees say so – and keep
them out. If they are, see how the classes can be
organized for them, and let them in. MR. STANSFELD
spoke effectively for, MR. HOPE against, unsexing
the Doctorate.
DR. PLAYFAIR spoke as one in a perplexity between
his constituents and his convictions.'   *20.6.1874*

Slow progress was made in obtaining medical

WOMAN'S TRIUMPH IN THE PROFESSIONS

MEDICINE

First Lady Doctor. 'HE IS SLEEPING NOW, AND IS CERTAINLY
RECOVERING. HE PROPOSED TO ME THIS MORNING.'
Second Lady Doctor. 'INDEED! HE WAS PROBABLY DELIRIOUS.'

Punch Almanack 1907

training and as late as 1876 the examiners of the Royal
College of Surgeons resigned in a body rather than
examine three of the women who had studied medicine
at Edinburgh for the diploma of midwives. In 1876,
Parliament passed an Enabling Bill authorizing all
medical corporations to examine women, notwith-
standing the terms of their Charters and the Irish
College of Physicians made immediate use of these
new powers, Sophia Jex-Blake and Edith Pechey
(another of the original Edinburgh students who had
already qualified at Berne University) taking degrees
there. In 1877 Elizabeth Garrett Anderson's request
that London University should open its examinations
to women was met and the battle was won, for the
London School of Medicine for Women had been
opened in 1874 and the Royal Free Hospital was

prepared to admit women, so that they could obtain
the necessary clinical experience.

Inevitably *Punch* found women doctors and dentists
comic; sometimes it was the incongruity of fragile and
attractive women tackling 'masculine' jobs and sometimes the 'mannishness' of the professional woman
which was found amusing; both themes are recurrent.

Punch reported in 1887 that women were to be
enabled to take diplomas in dentistry and celebrated
the event with verses 'To a Lady Dentist'.

> 'Lady Dentist, dear thou art,
> Thou hast stolen all my heart;
> Take too, I shall not repine,
> Modest molars such as mine;
> Draw them at thine own sweet will,
> Pain can come not from thy skill.
>
> Lady Dentist, fair to see,
> Are the forceps held by thee;
> Lest those pretty lips should pout,
> You may pull my eye-teeth out;
> I'm regardless of the pangs,
> When thy hand extracts the fangs.
>
> Lady Dentist, hear me pray
> Thou wilt visit me each day,
> Welcome is the hand that comes –
> Lightly hovering o'er my gums.
> Not a throne, love, could compare
> With thy operating chair.
>
> Lady Dentist, when in sooth
> You've extracted every tooth,
> Take me toothless to your arms,
> For the future will have charms;
> Artificial teeth shall be –
> Work for you and joy for me!'   *29.10.1887*

FEMALE DENTISTRY
'IT'S *NEARLY* OUT; BUT MY WRIST IS SO TIRED THAT
I MUST REALLY *REST* A BIT!'   *1.11.1879*

The woman barrister is found infrequently in *Punch*,
as the legal profession was not opened to women until
the passage of the Sex Disqualification (Removal) Act
in 1919, but she is foreshadowed from time to time.
She is first shown amongst 'The Ladies of the Creation'
in the 1853 Almanack and a coiffeur 'Suitable for
Ladies called to the Bar (as they soon will be, of
course)' is depicted in 1875. The opening of the
Universities to women made it possible for them to
study law and *Punch* supported their hopes to practice
as early as 1875, in an article, 'Ladies of the Long
Robe'.

'According to the London Correspondent of the
Liverpool Post:
    "Some time ago four ladies, who passed the

THE BARRISTER.
Punch Almanack 1853

LAW

Lady Solicitor. 'WHY DID YOU DISSUADE MISS BROWN FROM
BRINGING A BREACH OF PROMISE ACTION AGAINST TOM
JONES? SHE WOULD HAVE BEEN SURE TO WIN IT.' Lady Barrister.
'UNDOUBTEDLY. BUT HE IS NOW ENGAGED TO ME.'
Punch Almanack 1907

London University Examination for Women,
entered themselves in the chambers of well-known
barristers for the purpose of studying law."
"A purpose not only legal but laudable. . . . The
more employments fit for gentlemen that are
opened to ladies the better. Any such calling is
better than marriage accepted merely as a situation. . . . Increase of remunerative employment for
women would doubtless be attended with a
corresponding diminution of mercenary espousals,
and proportionately of actions for breach of
promise of marriage".'   *17.4.1875*

Whatever happened to the four young ladies
referred to, they certainly could not practice either as
barristers or solicitors. In the above quotation, *Punch*

shows some understanding of the evil effect of the marriage market upon both sexes, for if women had to suffer the indignity of waiting to be selected, men ran the risk of being accepted for mercenary reasons and with simulated affection only.

The 'break-through' for women came during the first world war, which markedly accentuated the developing tendency for women to work in occupations formerly the preserve of men. The psychological change was as important as the material one for women, instead of being opposed and frustrated in their attempts to improve and expand their working opportunities, became heroines overnight through their willingness to work in munition factories, public transport and so on. War-time *Punch* is full of drawings of women doing 'men's work'; the 'conductorette' helping Mr. Asquith on to the 'bus in the section on 'The Vote' (see p. 114) and the women ambulance drivers shown here are typical examples of the new type of woman worker.

In spite of the patriotic post-war renunciation of jobs in favour of demobilized troops and the slump which followed the post-war boom, the ground gained was never quite lost.

1st Lady Driver (*novice*) 'But what do you do if you have a breakdown?'
2nd ditto (*old hand*) 'Dead easy, my dear. Just send a wire to H.Q. You see, you have the whole British Army behind you if anything goes wrong.'
Punch Almanack 1918

The Vote

The Vote

'Coming events cast their shadows before', as the saying goes. A sustained campaign for the woman's vote was not launched until 1866 but in 1832 a Petition for the Vote from Mary Smith of Yorkshire was presented to Parliament by Henry Hunt, M.P.; women took part in the Anti-Corn Law agitation and Women's Political Associations were formed as part of the Chartist Movement. Indeed, the first draft of the Charter included women, but this was amended in favour of adult male suffrage. In 1848 *Punch* has a little drawing, 'How to Treat Female Chartists', showing the women fleeing before a stream of vermin.

In the 1850s the question of the woman's vote was raised with increasing frequency and in 1852 *Punch* has a paragraph on 'The Female Franchise', which reads:

'In the House of Commons speaking on Mr. Hume's Reform motion, Mr. Napier is reported to have said –
"It was proposed that the franchise should be given to all persons of twenty-one years of age, who laboured under no mental or legal disability. Why, then, as had been asked before, should ladies be excluded?"

HOW TO TREAT THE FEMALE CHARTISTS. *15.7.1848*

1. Because there is no evidence that any lady is 21 years of age; inasmuch as no lady will ever tell what her age is.
2. Because, as the poet says of the softer sex, "Angels are painted fair to look like them;" so that they are already painted fairly enough in all conscience.' *3.4.1852*

The campaign commenced in earnest with the Petition of 1866, signed by 1,499 women and presented to Parliament by John Stuart Mill. The following year Mill tried to amend the Reform Bill then before the House in favour of women. The use of the word 'persons' in the cartoon, 'Mill's Logic; or, Franchise for Females' has a certain significance, for the amendment moved by Mill was 'to leave out the word "man" in order to insert the word "person" instead thereof'. Mill's amendment failed and the next step taken was to plead in the Courts that the word 'man' could be interpreted so as to include 'woman'; it was ruled in 1868 that as the law stood, women were not entitled to vote (Chorlton v. Lings).

John Stuart Mill felt very strongly about 'The Subjection of Women'. The Victorians stylized the rôles of men and women in a way which, today, we

MILL'S LOGIC; OR, FRANCHISE FOR FEMALES
'PRAY CLEAR THE WAY, THERE, FOR THESE-A-PERSONS.'
30.3.1867

should consider very restrictive. It was generally be-
lieved that the average woman was contented with her
lot – a view which seems to be supported by the
Punch cartoon, 'The Ladies' Advocate' – and there is
no way of knowing how far this was true. (Is anyone
man or woman, contented with his lot, or are most
lives lived in a state of 'quiet desperation'?) As always,
it was the energetic minority which tried to change
society and many looked upon Mill as a 'crank'.

THE LADIES' ADVOCATE

MRS BULL. 'LOR, MR MILL! WHAT A LOVELY SPEECH YOU *DID* MAKE. I DO DECLARE I HADN'T THE SLIGHTEST NOTION THAT WE WERE SUCH MISERABLE CREATURES. NO ONE CAN SAY IT WAS *YOUR* FAULT THAT THE CASE BROKE DOWN.'   *1.6.1867*

Women gained the right to vote in municipal elections in 1869. It was always contended by the 'anti's' that women did not want the vote and would not use it if they had it. The *Punch* cartoon, 'A Brave Lady', shows that they were willing to use their vote in local affairs and also that the Secret Ballot Act of 1872 eased the situation for the timid. Before 1872 the view was often expressed that the secret ballot would be necessary if married women were to vote. *Punch* reflects current opinion:

> '. . . if married women are to vote, the Ballot will be indispensable. The ruffians accustomed to beat their wives are not incapacitated by their brutality from voting; and they would coerce them by intimidation. The ladies of the higher classes would, doubtless, many of them be bribed by their husbands in all manner of ways, and often in the most unblushing manner, unless we adopted the system of secret voting.'   *2.4.1870*

Punch, in the open letter to Mrs. Professor Fawcett already quoted from in the section on 'Women's Rights', says, 'I find now . . . that you go in for repealing the electoral disabilities of all women, married as well as single.' The Suffrage Societies were claiming the vote for women on the same terms as men, the current basis being the occupation or ownership of property. After the passing of Married Women's Property Acts from 1870 onwards it was possible to hold that this claim included a small number of married women but the doctrine of coverture prevailed. In 1872 the Courts ruled that married women, otherwise qualified, could not vote in municipal elections (Regina v. Harrald). This question of married women was a constant thorn in the flesh of the suffragists; it was felt impracticable to ask for parliamentary enfranchisement on a wider

'A BRAVE LADY'
(At a local Election)
Strong-minded Young Person (escorts the little Vicar and her Aunt to Vote).
'I'M *ASTONISHED* AT YOUR BEING NERVOUS *THIS* YEAR, AUNT!,
WHY, WE HAVE ONLY TO PUT OUR PAPERS IN A BOX!'   *23.11.1872*

legal basis than that applying to men, but even if a bill
were drafted specifically to include married women
fulfilling the necessary qualifications, inevitably the
majority would have been widows or spinsters, for the
widest category was that of householders and few
married women were householders. This laid the
women's claim open to the criticism that what *Punch*
called 'naughty persons' would get the vote while
respectable married women were excluded. This point
is taken up by *Punch* in 1872. Private Members' Bills
for women's suffrage were regularly introduced from
1870 onwards, the first sponsor being Jacob Bright,
brother of John Bright of Anti-Corn Law fame. The
'Ugly Rush' cartoon commemorates the rejection of

the first of these bills, which was drafted by Dr. Richard Pankhurst, later to be the husband of Emmeline Pankhurst (née Goulden), the militant leader. This cartoon, even more than that of 'The Ladies' Advocate', depicts the suffragists as ugly, bespectacled females, presumably spinsters; beautiful married women, one with a child, are standing in the background and taking no interest; the conclusion is obvious. In 1872 *Punch's* 'Essence of Parliament' records:

> 'Wednesday (May 1st) A Woman's Day. The ladies crowded the gallery to hear MR. JACOB BRIGHT try to stick up a Jacob's ladder for them to climb to power. He stated their case very agreeably. MR. BOUVERIE gave battle, and urged that though the proposal was now to give Votes to Single Women only (whereby very naughty persons would obtain a privilege denied to virtuous matrons), the next thing would be to give votes to wives, and then we should set ourselves against the heavenly law which declared that man and wife are one flesh – only the male half is to be Lord and Master. There was a good deal of fun in the debate. . .'   *11.5.1872*

'A good deal of fun' seems to have been a regular result of the women's suffrage bills debated in the House of Commons every year (excepting 1874) during the 1870s. *Punch's* 'Essence of Parliament' relating to the 1877 bill is prefixed by a drawing of geese, one labelled 'spinster' and another wearing widow's weeds. The entry starts:

> 'The admission of Petticoats to polling-places was hotly discussed till a quarter to six and then howled out. . .'   *16.6.1877*

AN 'UGLY RUSH!'
MR BULL. 'NOT IF I KNOW IT!'
28.5.1870

Those who did not wish to object to women's suffrage
on principle could always object to the drafting of a
particular bill on the grounds of the exclusion of
married women. As 'Smelfungus on Female Suffrage
(in answer to an inquiring Friend)' puts it:

'Yes, Sir, I do think the House did well to fling
out the Ladies' Bill. No, Sir, I don't object to
Female Suffrage at all. Quite the reverse. But I

hate half measures. MR. COURTNEY'S Bill was a half measure, Sir. It left out the married woman; the better half of mankind. Yes, Sir; and the better half of womankind too – I mean for electoral purposes.'   *22.3.1879*

One should not conclude from this that current opinion favoured votes for married women; these limited bills had much more support than a wider one would have had at the time. One of the main objections to any enfranchisement of women was that it would be 'the thin end of the wedge' and eventually married women would be included, which would cause dissension in the matrimonial home and be giving the vote to 'dependent creatures'. Presumably the dependency must have been economic dependency, otherwise there would scarcely have been dissension, but perhaps it is wrong to look for logic in the opposition to women's suffrage; many argued simultaneously that no woman should vote, that it would wreck marriages if married women voted and that particular bills were undesirable because they were not drafted widely enough to include married women. The real basis of objection was conventional belief in what was fit and proper.

The apex of the early efforts came in 1884, when William Woodall attempted to amend the Reform Bill of that year in favour of women, but was frustrated by Gladstone. *Punch's* mythical back-bencher, 'Toby M.P.', tells the story:

'House of Commons Mon. June 9
Woodall about the House again tonight. "Haven't had a moment of peace since I took up this conf- I mean this great cause of women's suffrage. Never knew till now the deathless persistency of women. Night and day she pursues me. Dread

"THE ANGEL IN 'THE HOUSE';" OR, THE RESULT OF FEMALE SUFFRAGE.

14.6.1884

the postman's knock; began of late to go out the
back way, but they're round there now. May as
well go out like ordinary householder who's paid
his taxes. Great mistake for single man to
undertake the work . . . L.B. (Lydia Becker) does
her best to keep the crowd off; but begin to
suspect L.B. herself. Wish it was over. Couldn't
survive another fortnight. . ."'   *21.6.1884*

Punch at this time had 'A troubled Dream of the
Future', which resulted in a cartoon entitled '"The
Angel in 'The House';" or the Result of Female

Suffrage.' The reference is to an immensely popular
poem by Coventry Patmore, 'The Angel in the House',
expressing the Victorian ideal of home and woman-
hood. The home was the retreat from the rat-race of
the business world, where the 'economic' man of the
time could throw off his cares and regain his humanity
in an environment full of sweetness and light. It was
the duty of the wife to provide this environment and
to do so she must be unsullied by the 'men's world'
of business and politics. Alas, this world 'Of life's kind
purposes pursued with order'd freedom sweet and
fair' could easily turn into a world of narrowness,
pettiness and frustration and the 'Angel' into a nagging
wife. A nice point in the *Punch* cartoon is that the
knitting beside the woman M.P. is a blue stocking.

After the defeat of the 1884 amendment, the
parliamentary fortunes of women's suffrage declined.
Apart from 1886, when a Women's Suffrage Bill
passed its Second Reading, the repeated attempts to
promote Private Members' Bills were frustrated by
the various devices which can be used against such
measures. As *Punch's* 'Essence of Parliament' records
in 1891, 'Business done. Women's Rights men dished.'
These failures harmed the cause, but in 1892 *Punch*
shows, in 'The Westminster Waxwork Show for the
Session', a 'Bill to Extend Parliamentary Franchise to
Women' promoted by Sir A. Rollit. Gladstone cir-
culated an open letter to Samuel Smith, M.P., in
opposition to Sir Albert Rollit's Bill. A *Punch* cartoon
of May 14th in which 'Miss Sarah Suffrage' features
records this opposition. Gladstone was further em-
barrassed by a show of spirit within the Women's
Liberal Federation. 1892 was election year and the
Council of the W.L.F. instructed their executive
committee to promote women's enfranchisement, but
'not to make it a test question at the approaching
election'. The truth of the matter is that the formation

'NOT AT HOME'

MISS SARAH SUFFRAGE (indignantly). 'OH! "*OUT*" IS HE!' EIGHT-
HOURS BILL (angrily). 'YUS!—AND HE WON'T GET "*IN*", IF I CAN
HELP IT!!'
(Mr GLADSTONE has lately published an unsympathetic Pamphlet on
'Female Suffrage', and has declined to receive a Deputation on the 'Eight
Hours Day' Question).   *14.5.1892*

of women's sections of the political parties in the 1880s
had led to divided loyalties. It had done a certain
amount of good in proving that women were not
politically inept but, as none of the political parties was
prepared to adopt the cause of women's suffrage and
loyalty to the party leader and programme was, of
course, expected, this development did little to help
the suffrage cause.

In 1897 a Bill promoted by an M.P. with the somewhat incredible name of Faithfull Begg passed its
Second Reading, but further progress was blocked.
Understandably, *Punch* paid more attention to the
Diamond Jubilee of Queen Victoria in that year than
to women's suffrage, but on 17th July, the 'Essence of
Parliament' refers to a Petition by Mr. Courtney complaining of 'Legislation reduced to mere game of
chance. . . . Just claims of women repeatedly and
insultingly postponed. . . .'

1897 saw a reorganization of the Women's Suffrage
Societies, all existing Societies devoted exclusively to
women's suffrage being grouped in a new federation,
the National Union of Women's Suffrage Societies.
The early leader of the movement, Lydia Becker, had
died in 1890. She had served the cause well as Secretary
of the Manchester Society, Parliamentary Agent and
editor of the *Women's Suffrage Journal*. Her successor
was Millicent Fawcett, who saw the whole campaign
through from start to finish. As Millicent Garrett she
was too young to sign the 1866 Petition which her
sister Elizabeth, along with Emily Davies, took to the
House of Commons. She survived in old age until
1929, thus witnessing the passage of the Representation
of the People (Equal Franchise) Act of the previous
year, which gave women the vote on equal terms with
men.

The movement for the women's vote was revitalized
by the formation of the Women's Social and Political
Union (W.S.P.U.) by Emmeline Pankhurst in 1903.
Punch, in 1905, shows a friendly attitude through a
celebrated cartoon by Bernard Partridge, 'The Dignity
of the Franchise'. This cartoon, which followed the
introduction of a women's suffrage bill by Bamford
Slack, is particularly interesting, as it typifies the class
reaction of many members of the constitutional
societies (as the older organizations came to be called,

THE DIGNITY OF THE FRANCHISE
QUALIFIED VOTER. 'AH, YOU MAY PAY RATES AN' TAXES, AN'
YOU MAY 'AVE RESPONSERBILITIES AN' ALL; BUT WHEN IT
COMES TO *VOTIN'*, YOU MUST LEAVE IT TO *US* MEN!'   *10.5.1905*

with the advent of the militant W.S.P.U.). This attitude had been current since 1884, when large numbers of illiterate farm labourers were given the vote. Many educated women bitterly resented being voteless while their gardeners and the beery type of workman shown in the cartoon could go to the polls. The middle-class nature of the women's suffrage movement alienated some working-class groups, but substantial support was received in particular from the I.L.P. and the Women's Co-operative Guild.

The W.S.P.U. was originally formed with the intention of organizing Labour women in the North, Mrs. Pankhurst being at the time a member of the I.L.P. The connection with the political left was quietly dropped when the move to London showed that upper- and middle-class support was available and in 1907 Mrs. Pankhurst and her eldest daughter, Christabel, left the I.L.P. The second daughter, Sylvia, remained faithful all her life to left-wing causes. (There was a third daughter, Adela, who was less prominent than her sisters in the movement and at that time, one surviving son.)

Emmeline Pethick-Lawrence became Treasurer of the W.S.P.U. in 1906 and she and her husband managed to collect incredible sums of money for the movement. The eventual breach in 1912 between the Pankhursts and Pethick-Lawrences is commemorated in *Punch* by a cartoon (not reproduced) showing one suffragette asking another, 'Are you a Peth or a Pank ?'

The dictatorial methods of the Pankhursts led to a split in the militant movement at the end of 1907, the more democratically-minded members forming the Women's Freedom League in 1908 under the Presidency of Mrs. Charlotte Despard. The W.F.L., although militant, was less extreme than the W.S.P.U. but equally imaginative in the tactics developed.

Attitudes which were radical in the 1860s had

THE SHRIEKING SISTER
THE SENSIBLE WOMAN. '*YOU
HELP OUR CAUSE? WHY, YOU'RE
ITS WORST ENEMY!*   *17.1.1906*

A TEMPORARY ENTANGLEMENT
Jos. Sedley . . . SIR H-NRY C-MB-LL
B-NN-RM-N *Becky Sharp* . . . THE
SUFFRAGETTE.
(The Prime Minister has promised to
receive a deputation on the subject of
Female Suffrage after Easter.—*Daily
Paper.*)   *18.4.1906*

become reasonably conventional by the twentieth
century and, compared with the W.S.P.U., members
of the older, constitutional, suffrage societies were
respectable. Another famous *Partridge* cartoon, 'The
Shrieking Sister' brings out this point.

The first militant disturbance was in 1905 when
Christabel Pankhurst and Annie Kenney (a cotton
worker) were arrested following a Liberal meeting in
the Manchester Free Trade Hall. The resultant
publicity was more effective than the years of patient
work by the constitutional societies had been; the
obvious conclusion was drawn by the Pankhurst
organization.

The advent of a Liberal Government at the end of
1905 and its sweeping victory at the polls in 1906
encouraged all reformist movements, including that

of women's suffrage. The prime minister, Sir Henry
Campbell-Bannerman, was thought to be not un-
friendly to the cause and in 1906 *Punch* records his
flirtation with the suffragettes with the cartoon, 'A
Temporary Entanglement'. Later in the same year, the
W.S.P.U. created a disturbance in the precincts of
Parliament, which *Punch* took note of in verse.

> 'Here's the Rime of the Ten Pioneers,
> Who, braving all masculine jeers
>   In a dare-devil manner
>   Uplifted their banner
> And went for the Commons and Peers.'

On being prosecuted and sentenced, the women all
refused to pay the fines imposed.

> 'Though the fines were not heavy,
>   They tropped in a bevy
> To jail with a jubilant face.'

Not everyone appreciated the heroism.

> 'But the rest of the sex we are told,
> Only laugh, when they should have condoled;
>   So it seems a bit silly
>   To go and eat skilly,
> And earn the repute of a Scold!' *31.10.1906*

The suffragettes, as the W.S.P.U. members were
named, did not concentrate soleiy on militancy. They
developed a new approach. They were not content to
enquire whether individual M.P.s favoured their
cause, but demanded 'Votes for Women' and 'The
Vote Now' from the Liberal government; they were
not prepared to rely on Private Members' Bills but
demanded a Government measure; they were not

THE LADIES' PAGEANT
MR ASQUITH. 'THIS IS NO PLACE FOR ME!'
29.6.1910

prepared to obey laws in the making of which they had no say. Very sensibly, they worked out tactics for by-elections for, by concentrating their forces on one constituency, they could make a greater impact than was possible at a general election.

Considerable imagination was shown in the use of pageantry and various peaceful methods of propaganda. All sorts of 'gimmicks' were developed – buttons, badges, comic postcards, playing cards and various games designed to advertise the movement.

Some of the best remembered episodes were the work of the Women's Freedom League, whose members were responsible for tax resistance, chaining themselves to the railings of the House of Commons and the distribution of leaflets from a balloon floating over London.

Militancy was relatively mild until 1909, when hunger-striking commenced. The authorities countered with forcible feeding, which resulted in a hardening of the attitude of the suffragettes and the resort to more extreme measures.

After 1908, when Asquith became Prime Minister, anti-suffragists began to organize, though much less extensively than the suffragists. Both groups tried to influence Asquith who, disliking the idea of women's suffrage, was able to play off the one against the other.

Punch, in 1910, shows a harassed Asquith endeavouring to avoid both groups of women and, indeed, he would very much have liked to avoid the whole question. This, however, was impossible, for the advent of the militants had stimulated the constitutional suffrage workers to greatly increased activity and there was a majority of suffragists both in the House of Commons and the Cabinet. In spite of this advantage, the political position of the suffragists was difficult. Not only was there an anti-suffrage premier, but both the Unionists and Liberals treated women's suffrage as an 'open' question. As *Punch* indicates (Rag-Time in the House), some curious partnerships were formed, Lloyd George and Balfour being suffragists while Asquith and Austin Chamberlain were 'Anti's'.

From 1908 onwards Mr. Asquith had been giving pledges that the House of Commons should be allowed to deal with women's suffrage and in 1908, 1910 and 1911 Private Members' Bills enfranchising women had passed their Second Reading. The two latter Bills were known as 'Conciliation' Bills, as they were promoted by an all-party 'Conciliation' Committee. The suffragettes called a truce to militancy while these two Bills were before the House, thus showing that they were not completely unreasonable. The third time a 'Conciliation' Bill was introduced, in 1912, it was undermined by Asquith's prior announcement of a Reform Bill for men only, to be capable of amendment in favour of women. The suffragettes were by then completely convinced of the Government's bad faith and resorted to window-smashing. The 1912 Bill failed its Second Reading for a number of reasons, one of which was reaction against suffragette violence.

RAG-TIME IN THE HOUSE
(SIR EDWARD GREY'S Woman Suffrage Amendment produced some
curious partnerships.) *29.1.1913*

At last, in January 1913, it seemed that the stage was set for the House of Commons to consider women's suffrage amendments to Asquith's Reform Bill, but alas! the Speaker ruled Sir Edward Grey's key amendment out-of-order and the Bill was withdrawn. After this fiasco Asquith promised facilities for yet another Private Members' Bill. *Punch* records its disgust with the cartoon, 'A Pleasure Deferred'.

In addition to the Bills mentioned above, an Adult Suffrage Bill had passed its Second Reading in 1909, so the House had on several occasions expressed itself in favour of the women's vote and by 1913 not only the women's societies but the general public were tired of Asquith's shilly-shallying, a view which *Punch* shared.

The number of police used against the suffragettes had its ridiculous side, particularly at a time when there was gun-running in Ireland and the Ulster Unionists were openly drilling. Picture galleries received special protection, especially after the slashing of the 'Rokeby Venus' at the National Gallery by Mary Richardson on 10th March, 1914.

Suffragette violence took a more serious turn after the disillusionment of 1913. The militants stopped at nothing, except endangering human life. Widespread arson was committed, empty buildings being fired. Justice was not only blind but the law was helpless, also. The suffragettes could not be kept in prison for they resorted to hunger-striking and when their health had broken down, so that their lives were endangered, they were released. Even the notorious 'Cat and Mouse Act' of 1913 was ineffective. Under this Act, prisoners could be released on health grounds and, when sufficiently recovered, re-arrested to serve the remainder of their sentences. Women suffered martyrdom in prison, but the most spectacular martyr was Emily Wilding Davison, who threw herself in front of the King's horse at the 1913 Derby and was killed.

The Majesty of the Law   *5.3.1913*

A PLEASURE DEFERRED
SUFFRAGIST. 'YOU'VE CUT MY
DANCE!' MR ASQUITH. 'YES, I
KNOW. THE FACT IS THE M.C.
OBJECTED TO THE PATTERN OF
MY WAISTCOAT, AND I HAD TO
GO HOME AND CHANGE IT.
BUT I'LL TELL YOU WHAT! LET
ME PUT YOU DOWN FOR AN
EXTRA AT OUR PRIVATE SUB-
SCRIPTION DANCE NEXT SEA-
SON!'   *5.2.1913*

THE MILITANT SCANDAL
I.—THE SKIED ARTIST COMES INTO HIS OWN
13.5.1914

*Militant Suffragist (after long and futile efforts to
light a fire for her tea-kettle)* 'And to think that only
yesterday I burnt two pavilions and a church.'
4.5.1913

Militant. 'Now isn't that provoking? Here's a lovely big house to let *and I've forgotten my matches!*' *2.7.1913*

Incendiarism generally and the setting fire to pillar-boxes in particular proved a double-edged weapon. The suffragettes showed that the law could be set at nought and the Liberal Government defied but in doing so they antagonized a large section of the public which, presumably, they hoped to convert to their cause.

Elaborate, but usually futile, precautions were taken to exclude suffragettes from public functions, particularly if a Cabinet Minister was to be present. Women became 'The Suspected Sex' and the police had a very difficult and embarrassing time. The prisoners included all classes of society and one of the interesting side-effects of the suffrage movement was the reform of women's prisons, due to the sentencing of articulate and spirited women and their revelation of prison conditions on their release.

THE SUSPECTED SEX

Girl (suddenly noticing policeman). 'I FAHND IT LIKE THAT. I NEVER
DONE IT, MISTER; STRAIGHT I NEVER!'   *16.7.1913*

The arson went on and on; public opinion hardened
against the suffragettes; the constitutional workers
who, in the early days, had occasionally been prepared
to present a united front with the militants, now felt
that their chances of success had been ruined by the
extreme militant violence. An *impasse* had been
reached, with more and more women enduring the
torture of the hunger-strike and forcible feeding. The
unfortunate Home Secretary, Reginald McKenna, was
inundated with suggestions on what to do with the
suffragettes. Favourites were that they should be
allowed to starve themselves to death or be deported
to the colonies. Apparently it was too simple to settle
the matter by giving the women what they wanted.
McKenna's attempt to deal with the problem by the
'Cat and Mouse Act' could scarcely be called a good

idea. It is difficult to respect an administration that did little to cope with practically open rebellion in Northern Ireland but subjected women demanding the vote to forcible feeding and the 'Cat and Mouse Act'. The deadlock was broken by the declaration of war in August, 1914. Millicent Fawcett sent a message to all branches of the National Union of Women's Suffrage Societies (of which she was President), ' Let us prove ourselves worthy of citizenship whether our claim be recognized or not'. The suffragettes also rallied to their country; the prisoners were released and Christabel Pankhurst (who, since 1912, had been running the movement from Paris after escaping arrest) returned from exile.

Women's war work was a wonderful 'face-saver' for those who wished to drop their opposition to women's

ÆSCULAPIUS IN LONDON
MR McKENNA (to Presiding Deity of International Medical Congress) 'YOU LOOK AS IF YOU KNEW ALL ABOUT MICROBES, SIR. COULDN'T YOU FIND ME AN ANTIDOTE TO THIS?'   *13.8.1913*

THE CATCH OF THE SEASON
Conductorette (*to Mr Asquith*). 'COME ALONG SIR. BETTER LATE THAN NEVER'   *4.4.1917*

suffrage, either because they had genuinely changed their minds or because they did not wish to face a renewal of militancy after the war. Even Mr. Asquith, whom the women considered their greatest enemy, at last proclaimed himself converted.

After a Speaker's conference on Electoral Reform had recommended in their favour, women over thirty who were householders or the wives of householders, or who held graduate qualifications, were enfranchised in 1918. In 1928 the franchise was equalized between men and women; so ended the most protracted and dramatic campaign of the women's emancipation movement.

AT LAST! *23.1.1918*

Epilogue

Epilogue

A hundred years on from the formation of the first societies for women's suffrage, it is interesting to see how *Punch* reflects the life of the modern, emancipated woman. *Punch* itself has changed its nature as the result of women's emancipation, many of its present-day contributors being women who can afford to laugh at themselves. During the campaign, the strain was so great and the stakes played for so high that the feminists were inclined to treat themselves and their cause with a deadly earnestness; now, although there is still some 'unfinished business', women can afford to take a more relaxed attitude and treat their position with a sense of humour.

Glancing back at the issues dealt with in the previous pages, it is interesting to find that 'Women and Work' is still a 'live' subject for *Punch* in the 1960s, while 'Education' and 'The Vote' have died a natural death, being no longer news. No doubt this is because the goals of 'Equal Pay' and 'Equal Opportunity' in the sphere of employment have not yet been attained. A woman captain of a ship is news today and *Punch* celebrated the arrival of the Russian liner *Alexander Pushkin* with an article by Alexander Frater, *The Skipper, She's a Lady*. (27.4.1966). The Captain is described as 'a stocky blonde in gum boots and house

Both parents working—O.K.?   *26.5.1965*

coat'. 'Where have you come from?' the interviewer asked her. 'I cannot say', she said slipping an *eau de cologne* spray beneath her house coat and pumping.

The modern story is not simply that of women storming male strongholds; in *Sex Barrier Finally Smashed*, Angela Milne discusses the appointment of a male nurse as Matron of a Glamorgan hospital, quoting his comment, 'This is quite a break-through'. (22.7.1964).

The early feminists had the spinster, the widow and

the deserted wife in mind when they demanded the
right to work; the problem was to find employment,
particularly for middle-class women, which would
bring in a competence. Today the problem is that
married women comprise over half the female labour
force and face the difficulty of reconciling claims of
home and claims of work. Women have gained many
new jobs but have not lost their old ones and many of
the articles by women contributors to *Punch* reflect
this dichotomy. *A Day in the Life of Monica Furlong*
illustrates this admirably:

'The problem is that professionally I have one
complete set of hurdles and that as a mother I
have a different set, and that if I am not quick and
clever I am jumping in all directions at once.
As a professional journalist my duties are clear.
I must read the newspapers thoroughly, read the
new books and pamphlets which relate to my
subjects, answer my letters, keep my appoint-
ments, visit the offices of the paper I work for,
and remain on affable terms with a number of
people. Besides turning in copy from time to time.
As a wife and mother I am in a different case.
There the brief is partly a listening one – a matter
of sympathizing over the ghastly trains, the in-
competence of everyone, the beastliness of
teachers and the intractability of homework. It
means turning myself into a kind of conveyor-belt
of clean clothes, food, cough medicine, aspirin,
electric light bulbs, money for church collection,
money for charity, money for outings, toothpaste,
toilet-paper, Kleenex tissues, and interesting
things to do on cold, wet afternoons. It means
continually transporting someone somewhere – my
son to get his hair cut, my daughter to ballet, the
cat to the vet. It means remembering to get a new

'Always on the go, these married ex-teachers. Either forgotten to put the
laundry out, left something in the oven, haven't fed the cat . . .'   *24.3.1965*

element for the gaslighter, some de-icer for the
windscreen and a new set of name-tapes for the
beginning of term. (It adds up to a heavy programme of embracing, soothing, loving, telling
stories, running baths, bathing flesh wounds, and
carrying out improvised visits to the Science
Museum.)

Now I don't wish to complain over my lot – indeed
since I am very largely the architect of it, there
would be little point in doing so. Nevertheless
the thing which is quite clear to me about "My
Day" is that it is a physical impossibility.

Journalism, properly carried out, is a full-time
job. It ought to be. Wife and motherhood is a

full-time job. What, then, am I doing? Believe me, I often wonder, especially when the conflicting demands come. What I could do with myself, I sometimes think grimly, as a wife—the old-fashioned dedicated kind, with not a thought in her head but housewifery and balancing her slender budget.

And why am I not like that myself? I suppose because, whatever they say about women, I prefer abstract ideas to concrete ones. I use words happily and domestic tools diffidently, and it seems madness, therefore, to abandon writing for housework. Yet I could no more live without family life than a turtle-dove could exist happily, deprived of her cock and young ones.'   *23.3.1966*

The cartoon of the racing married women teachers makes the same point. A little cynicism is brought to bear on the subject by a skit entitled 'Guide to Dreamland', inspired by a news item:

'The Pharmaceutical Society is investigating reports that young people are buying packets of Morning Glory seed by the gross to make an hallucinatory drug. They had better get on with it. There are plenty of other things awaiting their attention.
. . . . Citrone, a drug derived from strained parsnips. . . . the drug is clinically useful in deluding intelligent women into the acceptance of their role as housewife and mother as a full and worthwhile life.'   *30.3.1966*

Occasionally the gaff is blown by a woman herself. Hazel Townson, in *Working it out* writes:

'Despite all the highfalutin talk we've had on the

She's a woman of few ideas, but they always become rich husbands.   *3.3.1965*

subject lately, it's *cunning* that makes mothers of young families go out to work. . . .'   *19.1.1966*

The superior money-making opportunities of the average man have left a situation where, if money grabbing is the main object, it is just as reasonable for a woman to try to find a rich husband as to embark upon an arduous career. (Fortunately, not all women are mercenary – also there is a certain shortage of rich husbands.) Almost every woman who has tried to combine marriage and a career has wondered why she bothers. Penelope Mortimer, describing the trials of a novelist, writes:

> 'All you need is a . . . ruthless egoism – or the good sense to take up some other, more practical career, such as marrying for money.'
>
> *Genesis of a Novel* (*13.4.1966*)

She also explains how the tensions of domestic life can build up a need for release – a need more capable of being met today than in days gone by, although the 'break-through' of women novelists preceded the emancipation movement.

> 'Marriage, having children, the whole domestic experience, provided no alternative to writing; on the contrary they created a situation in which writing became absolutely essential. . . . Briefly, if you bottle something up, confine it, force the quart into the pint bottle, release is essential; if, on the other hand there is no conflict, no limitation, no pressure, the need becomes sluggish, shallow and diffused.'

It is now possible for women to take the whole business of marriage in a different spirit from that which prevailed a hundred years ago. Then, to the middle-class woman, a husband was a desperately needed meal-ticket and status symbol; this gave an unhealthy edge to the natural desire, shared by men and women, to find a suitable mate. Now that not only the status of women has changed but also the sex ratio, the still important question of a husband has resolved itself into finding a suitable partner in a context of more males under 30 years of age than females. This situation, combined with the ability of most women to maintain themselves adequately by their own efforts,

Little did they think, when I posed them for this group picture,
that I was going to marry them all. *21.4.1965*

has brought a lighter touch to the subject of matrimony. As ever, *Punch* finds much to laugh at in
marriage, but a frivolous approach to the question of
changing partners, as shown by the cartoons of the
much-marrying women, is relatively new.

The suffragettes thought that once women obtained
the vote there would be a brave new world and an end
to the exploitation of sex. The Strip Clubs of today,
featured in modern *Punch*, would have horrified them.

Emancipation from Victorian prudery was not one
of the objects of the Womens' Rights movement; the

I've never been to a place like this before. It's a bit like my first day at school. *16.7.1965*

campaign against a double standard of morality was inspired by the wish to raise the standard of men to that of respectable women.

Neither the hopes of the feminists nor the fears of the anti-feminists have been fully realized; nevertheless, the 'Women's Rights Movement' (aided by economic and social developments not directly connected with it) has been a success; the vote has been obtained and women of today have many more opportunities than a hundred years ago. The male anti-feminists were afraid that woman (they always spoke of 'woman'), if emancipated, would lose her feminity and attraction. She has not done that, as *Punch* shows. The lady opposite is somewhat obviously *not* 'Burlington Bertie', in spite of her affirmation to that effect.

I'm Burlington Bertie . . .   *10.3.1965*

Perhaps there was a little justification in the anti-feminist fear that women, on entering a man's world, would become more like men; there has been a blurring of the line which used to demarcate the functions of the sexes and modern young married couples often have an accommodating domestic partnership, rather than a rigid division of labour between the sexes.

What are we to make of the old fear that women would come to resemble men, when we look at the young people of today, so similar with their long hair and jeans? This is certainly no result of the Women's Rights movement and is due more to a change in male fashion than to anything else. Perhaps men have become tired of their conventional rôle and appearance and have decided to be emancipated too.

Same old story—boy meets girl but doesn't know it.   *6.4.1966*